PROBLEMS IN LATIN AMERICAN CIVILIZATION

The Bourbon Reformers and Spanish Civilization

TROY S. FLOYD

D. C. Heath and Company

THE BOURBON REFORMERS
AND SPANISH CIVILIZATION

Builders or Destroyers?

PROBLEMS IN LATIN AMERICAN CIVILIZATION

UNDER THE EDITORIAL DIRECTION OF
EDWIN LIEUWEN, UNIVERSITY OF NEW MEXICO

INDIAN LABOR IN THE SPANISH INDIES — Was There Another Solution? — *Edited by John Francis Bannon, S.J., Saint Louis University*

THE BOURBON REFORMERS AND SPANISH CIVILIZATION — Builders or Destroyers? — *Edited by Troy S. Floyd, University of New Mexico*

Other volumes in preparation

PROBLEMS IN LATIN AMERICAN CIVILIZATION

THE BOURBON REFORMERS
AND SPANISH CIVILIZATION

Builders or Destroyers?

EDITED AND TRANSLATED WITH AN INTRODUCTION BY

Troy S. Floyd UNIVERSITY OF NEW MEXICO

D. C. HEATH AND COMPANY · BOSTON

Library of Congress Catalog Card Number 66-26811

COPYRIGHT © 1966 BY D. C. HEATH AND COMPANY

BOSTON   ENGLEWOOD   CHICAGO   DALLAS   SAN FRANCISCO   ATLANTA

PRINTED IN THE UNITED STATES OF AMERICA

PRINTED JULY 1966

Table of Contents

Introduction

FOR Spain the eighteenth century began and ended with crisis. When Charles II, the last Habsburg monarch, died in 1700, the North European powers planned to partition the Spanish Empire. Faced with political extinction, Spain turned to the dominant power, France, and invited Philip, grandson of Louis XIV, to ascend the Spanish throne. Although Philip founded the Spanish Bourbon dynasty the next year, Spain was obliged to pay a high price for casting her fortunes with France. England was determined that two large nations should not be united against her, and with the support of several small powers, declared war against the Bourbons in 1703. When the war ended a decade later with the signing of the Treaty of Utrecht, Spain lost her European holdings but was permitted to retain the Bourbon monarchy, provided that Spain and France were never ruled by a single monarch. Although suffering painful losses, Spain had survived the first crisis and continued to survive — thanks to reforms — in the years following. It was not until 1793 that Spain again faced an enemy on her own soil. Revolutionary France invaded her former ally, who had signed an alliance with England, and obliged Spain to sign the Peace of Basle in 1795. But changing sides only hastened the crisis, for Spain was no match for England, and had to be saved by that power when Napoleon turned on his weak ally in 1808, invaded the country, and occupied it until driven out six years later.

Between these two crises there was occurring gradually but profoundly a crisis of a very different kind. This was a crisis in values brought about by the rise of a new kind of Spaniard, in Spain and America, who challenged the traditional Spanish assumptions about the meaning of material progress, liberty, and faith. This challenge was revealed in the eighteenth century mainly in verbal conflict. But in the nineteenth and twentieth centuries, the crisis was manifest in the many civil wars in Spain and in her former Empire, where conservatives and liberals, centralists and federalists, proclericals and anticlericals tried to settle by force what the eighteenth century could not settle by debate. It is obvious that Spanish civilization was, and still is, in crisis and that the conflict originated in the eighteenth century.

This crisis of values is reflected in contemporary and retrospective writings. Eighteenth-century writers praised or blamed the Bourbon Government for what it had or had not done, and later historians eulogized or condemned the government in the light of present conditions in their country, which they attributed to the influence of the former Spanish monarchs. Were the Bourbons constructive reformers who kept the best of traditional Spanish civilization while appropriating from Western Europe the best ideas and techniques for material development? Or did they unconsciously preside over the dissolution of Spanish civilization because they tolerated anything except limitation of their own power? Whatever the answers may be to these questions, it is certain that the Bourbons have been held responsible for what they did, failed to do, or merely permitted.

The literature of this controversy, represented in the readings below, cannot be understood apart from some broad considerations about traditional Spanish civilization, the new ideas of the eighteenth century, and the relation of the Bourbon reforms to both old and new ideas. This is especially true because the writers were not trying to explain the crisis to an uninformed world; they usually wrote in the white heat, or at least the red afterglow, of civil wars in which thousands perished to preserve what each side believed was worth preserving. Although material progress, liberty, and faith were not separate issues in the historical controversy, it is hardly possible to discuss them except separately.

Europe was much concerned with material progress in the eighteenth century. Until approximately the last quarter of the century, however, governments were almost exclusively concerned with material progress as a means of strengthening the State, mainly because weakness invited an attack from naval powers. Mercantilism was the time-honored method for building state power through the state-controlled production of raw materials, manufacturing, and trade. Since France had risen to primacy by the efficient practice of mercantilism, it was to France that the Bourbon reformers turned.

The first half of the century was characterized by trial and error, and only indifferent results. José Patiño, one of the first able reforming ministers, rebuilt the Spanish navy and expanded the merchant marine as the result of a series of measures passed during the second and third decades of the century. The government subsidized textile factories in Spain and granted to monopoly companies the right to develop cotton, cacao, sugar, tobacco, and other products in various parts of America. The most successful of these monopoly companies was the Guipúzcoa (Caracas) Company, chartered in 1728, which greatly increased the production of cacao in Venezuela. Meanwhile the Spanish _flota_, which had sailed more or less annually to the Indies since the sixteenth century, continued to call at its main ports — Cartagena, Portobelo, and Veracruz. But the day of the monopoly company and the annual fleet system was nearly over. Northern Europe was moving toward the industrial revolution, and manufactured goods were increasingly more plentiful both in Europe and in the American colonies of these manufacturing powers. Some of these colonies — such as Jamaica, Curaçao, and Martinique — were virtual _entrepôts_ for smuggling with the Spanish Americans. The annual fleet found virtually no demand for its limited, high-priced goods; consequently, in 1748 the part of the fleet calling at Cartagena-Portobelo was abolished.

The Bourbon reformers were aware of the shortcomings in the old methods of mercantilism and were ready to make sweeping changes. In 1765 a decree opened most of the Spanish Caribbean island ports to "free trade" with a half-dozen Spanish ports. By this decree, individual ships could sail to these privileged ports under a reduced tax schedule. The production of sugar and other tropical products rose rapidly. In 1774 another decree permitted the parts of the Empire from Mexico to Chile to trade with each other by way of the Pacific. Finally, in 1778, came the most important of the trade reforms — the Free Trade Reglamento — which permitted free trade in virtually the whole Empire, opening many new ports in America and Spain and making further reductions in the taxes on commerce. As a result, the production of raw materials in Spanish America during the last quarter of the eighteenth century reached the highest levels of the colonial period. Spanish merchants were encouraged by the Crown to emigrate to America where they were instrumental in expanding production and trade. The bulk of the trade was with Cádiz, the only legal port until 1764, and still the leading one thereafter. Expanded trade made possible the establishment of new _consulados_ (merchant guilds) in Chile, Cartagena, Buenos Aires, and Guatemala in the 1790's and was responsible for the rise of a new class, the Spanish bourgeoisie, who challenged the Old Regime in many ways.

That the Bourbons were builders of civilization in its material aspects is unquestionable. What they destroyed of traditional Spanish civilization is less certain, but doubtless the peace of mind that rests on indifference to the conditions of life was shattered. The crisis in Spanish civilization emerged, however, not only from the example of rapid change furnished by the Bourbons, but even more from the dream of eighteenth-century liberals that great material progress would come about as the cumulative result of individual efforts unhindered by direction of the State. Progress, like liberty, was to be by and for the people. It was this dream that contributed to later conflict because the failure of its realization was blamed on the government or the party in power or the foreign exploiter. Progress was humanly possible. If it produced negligible results certain human beings were always to be judged guilty.

The spread of material progress by the Bourbons was uneven; it was of great benefit to certain regions and to certain groups but left other regions and classes, especially the lower classes, virtually untouched. The narrow and shallow quality of progress is revealed in the first section of readings. The author of the first selection, Tomás Lurquín, a merchant in Santiago de Chile, believed the Bourbon monarchs were the torchbearers of a progress soon to spread over the entire Empire. Writing in 1801 when peace in the Napoleonic Wars (1793–1815) was expected, he saw great possibilities for the marketing of Chilean copper, wheat and other products in Spain and the Empire. In the second selection the conservative Venezuelan historian, Angel César Rivas, likewise pays tribute to the Bourbons as leaders of material progress. Rivas argues, from the perspective of the early twentieth century, that the Bourbons laid the material base for the flourishing of the brilliant generation of independence leaders. Others writers have charged, however, that the economic reforms lacked breadth and depth. In 1812, Miguel Ramos Arizpe, a priest from northeastern Mexico, argued before the Spanish *Cortes* (national assembly) that the reforms had never reached his region; its inhabitants were forced to buy manufactures at exorbitant prices and to sell raw materials for a pittance. He hinted that an independence movement, more serious than the current one in Mexico, would result if

reforms were not soon made in the Northeast. Far more critical for traditional Spanish society was the accusation made in 1799 by Manuel Abad y Queipo, a Spanish priest living in Michoacán, central Mexico. Grieved because the Indians and *mestizos,* who made up the great majority of the population in his region, were isolated, ignorant, and miserable in this century of progress, he predicted that unless the Crown won their loyalty by "ties of interest," they would probably rebel for they had nothing to lose by such action. In this idea — that all society must be included in the benefits of material progress — lay the seeds of dissolution of traditional Spanish civilization. Although he was not a revolutionary Abad had advanced an idea that became part of liberal reform. It was written into law in the land reform programs of Mexico and Spain in the middle of the nineteenth century, and has been a main issue in twentieth-century revolutions.

The second aspect of the crisis, which reflected rising aspirations for liberty, was in its immediate effects even more disruptive than the issue of progress. Contrary to what might be supposed, the crisis did not arise merely from the conflict between Enlightened Despotism and individual freedom. Rather, it reflected a clash between the champions of two specific kinds of liberty, the traditional Spanish liberty and the individual liberty of the eighteenth century.

Traditional Spanish liberty had its roots in the Roman city-state and in medieval civilization. It was specific and limited; the several political and civil liberties were enumerated in charters and granted by the king. Called *fueros,* these privileges were granted to cities, kingdoms, merchant guilds, the clergy, and other groups or institutions — not to individuals. This system encouraged and helped support a civilization in which persons regarded themselves as belonging to some group or small political entity. Resulting, at its best, in a harmonious balance of parts under a king whose main role was to dispense justice, it also permitted a few men to exercise power over the small, passive population in each part. It was a political system that worked well for a relatively static society.

The individualist philosophy of the Enlightenment defined liberty as the right of every man to vote, to hold political office, and to share in the law-making process without reference to what group he belonged to or to any other traditional consideration. This idea had great appeal to those Spaniards and Spanish Americans who could expect little from traditional liberties because they were second sons, impoverished petty nobles, or members of the new merchant class.

For a time, the profound differences between the two kinds of liberty were obscured by the fact that supporters on both sides used the same vocabulary to express their ideas. The Wars for Independence were fought for both kinds of liberty and the victors afterward fell into civil war when the advocates of the two kinds of liberty realized how far apart they were from each other.

The Bourbon political reforms, which sharply subordinated liberty to security and progress, were against both kinds of liberty, the old and the new. As the selection by Vicente Palacio Atard makes clear, the centralization of political power by the Bourbons was not owing to a change in the theory of monarchical government. A reduction of the liberties formerly enjoyed by various institutions was the result of the establishment of centralized bureaucracy which could organize and direct the many political and economic reforms. In Spain, several councils that had formerly advised the king were abolished or left idle; a half-dozen ministers, appointees of the king, now administered the important business of the Empire. The Kingdom of Aragón, most important of the old autonomous kingdoms, lost its *fueros* because it had opposed the Bourbon king in the War of the Spanish Succession. Municipal government in Spain and America tended to decline in importance as intendants subjected the

cities to close supervision. Partly because the eighteenth century was marked by a half-dozen imperial wars, the Bourbons relied heavily upon military men who governed stiffly, exercising all power because of the continual state of emergency. It was true that such officials saved the Empire from conquest, as at Cartagena in 1741 where the British were repulsed, and that they expanded the Empire into Uruguay, Texas, and California. But if centralization of power produced prosperity and security and a larger empire, it nonetheless reduced the area of private liberty. To do this in a century when most men aspired to greater liberty than Western civilization had ever permitted was to create an unbearable tension.

For this reason it is understandable that neither the advocates of traditional liberty nor those of individual liberty have praised the Bourbons. But the traditionalists, called *Hispanistas* by their opponents in Spanish America, have moderated their criticism, mainly on the grounds that traditional liberty was so deeply rooted in the Spanish character that the Bourbons could not extinguish it. This view has put them at odds with the view of the *nacionalistas* that genuine liberty was foreign to Spanish civilization. As the readings of the second section indicate, not only a different understanding of liberty, but the special circumstances of a region and the evaluation of their own nineteenth-century history influence the writers' points of view. The protest made to the *Cortes* of Cádiz in 1812 by the Mexican priest, Miguel Ramos Arizpe, previously mentioned, is representative of the liberal-nationalist school of thought that dominated Latin American history in the nineteenth century. In the first selection of the section on liberty, Ramos Arizpe charges that the four provinces of the Northeast were under a system of military despotism affording no opportunity for the exercise of liberty by the people. His reference to the sacred rights of man identifies him as a "new Spaniard," whose ideas could not be reconciled even with pre-Bourbon Spain. In the second selection, the liberal, Enrique Bernardo Núñez, writing in 1948 after a half century of dictatorship in Venezuela, holds that liberty had been impossible under the Spanish at any time, and that the independence movement could be explained by a universal desire of the downtrodden to "throw off the yoke."

The next three selections are concerned with the state of traditional Spanish liberty under the Bourbons. In a moving peroration, the traditionalist Venezuelan Rivas contends that the idea of liberty, inseparably part of the Spanish character, could only be curtailed, not extinguished by the Bourbons; it had existed in municipal government both in Spain and in Venezuela until the eighteenth century, and it was recovered, as the Spanish race would always recover it, by the opportunity that followed the Napoleonic invasion of 1808. One of the most penetrating analyses of the state of liberty under the Bourbons is that made in the next selection by a twentieth-century Spanish historian, Vicente Palacio Atard. No selection implies more strongly that the crisis which Spanish civilization has since been facing is between the traditional meaning of liberty and the modern one. Because of their failure to expand, even to retain, the institutional liberties, Palacio Atard apparently holds the Bourbons responsible for inspiring in some Spaniards, by their bad example, such a hatred for authority that anarchy and other forms of extreme liberty have plagued Spain ever since. The granting of moderate liberty, he indicates, might have saved a century of bloodshed — a contention understandable in one who has lived through the Spanish civil war of 1936–39. In the final reading, the Chilean professor Jaime Eyzaguirre, writing in 1957, refutes the liberal view that the Bourbons were despotic by showing that creoles [native-born whites] held more than fifty percent of the positions in the colonial bureaucracy in the immediate pre-independence years. But Chile was perhaps unique in Spanish America in returning after independence to a traditional Spanish liberty that was not for some time seriously challenged by the new Liberals. Elsewhere, new and old and confused ideas of liberty were the banners of military leaders. Thus it seems likely that the liberal hatred of Bourbon despotism would not have been abated by office-holding. The aspiration for individual liberty went far beyond this.

The third and final aspect of the crisis in Spanish civilization is the conflict between faith and liberty. A profound faith in Catholic Christianity is probably the most deeply-rooted value in Spanish civilization. The Spanish people acquired their national self-consciousness as a result of eight centuries of conflict against the Moors (711–1492), and deepened their faith by the great experience of spreading it across two thirds of the Western hemisphere, defending it for two centuries in Europe, and protecting it by the Inquisition in their own civilization. Out of this long process emerged a powerful and influential church which had in its care the conscience and mind and spirit of the civilization.

Nothing could have more sharply divided Spanish civilization than the rise of a group of intellectuals who seized hold of a new idea, antagonistic to traditional civilization based on the church, which inspired in them all the steadfast faith, courage, and energy that their forebears had given to a militant Christianity. We refer here to the Spanish and Spanish American liberals, new men, born of the eighteenth-century Enlightenment; its conception of individual liberty appealed immensely to an inherent Spanish trait of individualism called variously, Moorish, Arabic, and Levantine. But it was not so much political liberty as it was liberty of conscience that brought the new liberal into conflict with the church. Although the liberal was not anti-religious, he preferred — perhaps because conquest of the external world for Christianity was no longer possible — to make his own conquest of the spirit. Perhaps he would rather find

God or risk damnation by his own free will than be ushered into Heaven on the arm of authority. Believing himself free, he opposed anything restricting his freedom of expression, and he demanded a free society in which truth must stand the repeated test of free discussion.

Between these two extreme positions — that of the free-thinking liberal and that of the authoritarian church, the Bourbon government held a position somewhat left of center. The Bourbon ministries were not primarily concerned with freedom of conscience. But they were concerned with promoting higher education in the sciences in order that university graduates would be qualified to supervise material development of the Empire. They were also concerned with encouraging the study of the political and economic philosophies of the progressive North European countries in order that useful ideas might be found for the good of the State. For these reasons they relaxed censorship of imported books, and permitted the establishment of groups called Sociedades who freely discussed the new ideas and made innumerable scientific experiments. Among the new ideas was utilitarianism — a philosophy which held that the greatest happiness for the greatest number was to be achieved by the individual following his own interest. Because the whole range of ideas from a Europe in ferment came into Spain and Spanish America along with the useful knowledge which the Bourbons desired, the church became suspicious that the government was, if not impious, at least criminally careless.

In this atmosphere, the church could not help viewing certain acts by the Bourbon Government as positively anti-clerical. Many of the clergy believed the expulsion of the Jesuits in 1767 was merely symptomatic of a new secular monarchy, which then took over collection of the tithes in 1774 and later imposed taxes on the clergy. But it was in education where the great crisis between liberty and faith was first revealed. Although the Bourbon Government did not generally exclude the clergy from teaching, the Liberals tended to seize the leadership, teaching the new philosophy with all its implications for the faith and morals of which the clergy had been sole custodian. Liberty of conscience and freedom of discussion were in this way pitted against a faith long closely associated with authority, and this issue has been involved in the majority of the civil wars fought in Spain and Spanish America to the present day.

The last section of readings illustrates how the Bourbon reformers have been judged on the question of the church in a liberal society. The first two readings, in which judgment of the Bourbons is more implied than stated, are concerned with a specific question rising out of this controversy in post-independence Colombia. Among the autonomous theories of ethics and morals much beloved by the eighteenth-century *philosophes* was the self-interest theory. Present in various philosophies, this theory was part of the utilitarianism of Jeremy Bentham, whose work on legislation became the textbook for the study of law in the colleges of Bogotá. In the first reading, Doctor Vicente Azuero, a Colombian liberal, writing in 1826, praises Bentham's work as admirably suitable for an individualist society. But the same work is roundly condemned in the second selection by José Manuel Groot, a Colombian historian writing in the 1860's, who argues that sensual man would commit spiritual suicide if he were taught to pursue his self-interest. Groot's vehemence is understandable because he had lived through years of bloody civil wars between liberals and conservatives and was convinced that a secular view of life was daily destroying the religiosity of Colombia. Corruptible human nature, in this view, is hopelessly lost without the restraint of religion.

In the third selection, the Jesuit historian Mariano Cuevas charges that the cancerous disease of secularism and impiety came to Mexico about 1765 because of the criminal carelessness of Charles III and his ministers, who weakened the Inquisition and opened Mexico to a stream of heretical foreigners and impious books. In the last selection, however, the twentieth-century Spanish historian, Juan Manuel Herrero, takes a more sympathetic view of the Spanish liberals of the eighteenth century. Although he appreciates that they wished to make the clergy socially useful and enlightened, Herrero believes the pursuit of happiness, a main tenet of liberalism, could never be elevated above the faith without sacrificing the latter. He argues that the liberals were responsible for a decline of the faith in Spanish society because they advocated that religion contributes to happiness instead of holding fast to the traditional belief that a meaningful happiness is possible only as the result of religious faith.

The historical debate over the Bourbons is both complex and enduring. In essence, it turns on the impossibility of completely reconciling a profound concern for liberty of conscience with an equally profound concern for unity of faith. Without the former, liberals believe meaningful material progress is impossible; without the latter, religious conservatives contend that progress is only material and hence meaningless. In successfully meeting their security problems and in ably supporting material progress, the Bourbon reformers restricted liberty and appeared indifferent, even antagonistic to the Church. As the student reads the selections that follow, he will recognize that the conflicts about material progress, liberty, and faith in Spanish civilization are part of a conflict present, in varied form, in any modern society — his own and others.

[NOTE: All translations and all footnotes are by the editor. Footnotes which appeared in the original selections have been omitted for reasons of space.]

Chronology

1700   Philip V (1700–46), of French birth, inaugurates the Bourbon dynasty in Spain.

1718   Cádiz replaces Seville as the only port permitted to trade with Spanish America.

1721   Spanish begin the occupation of Texas to forestall French encroachment.

1726   Spanish found Montevideo as a buffer to the Portuguese.

1726   José Patiño, first of the able Spanish reforming ministers, becomes Minister of the Indies.

1728   Founding of the Caracas Company, by which Basques were granted a monopoly of trade for part of Venezuela.

1735   Individual register ships permitted to sail from Spain to various ports of Spanish America.

1739   Viceroyalty of New Granada, temporarily established 1717–1723, is definitely established.

1741   Some 20,000 British troops repulsed at Cartagena during the War of Jenkins' Ear.

1746   Ferdinand VI (1746–1759).

1748   Abolition of the galleons to Panama, marking ultimate replacement of the fleet system by individual ships.

1754   Spain signs a Concordat with the Vatican, making the Spanish Church practically independent of Rome. Tighter political control in age of dawning secularism heralds church-state conflict.

1756   Barcelona company granted trading rights in the Caribbean, especially stimulating the cotton trade in Eastern Venezuela.

1759   Charles III (1759–1788), in whose reign reforms in Spanish America reached a peak of intensity.

1761   Spain enters the Seven Years' War on the side of France.

1762   France cedes the Louisiana territory to Spain.

1763   Treaty of Paris. Spain cedes Florida to Great Britain in return for Havana and Manila, occupied by the British during the war.

1764   Intendancy system extended to Spanish America, beginning with Cuba; gradually instituted during the next three decades throughout most of the continental dominions.

1765   Direct trade authorized between the Spanish Caribbean and some half dozen ports of Spain.

1765   Foundation of a colonial militia begun with the organization, training, and equipping of native-born troops in the several Spanish American dominions.

1767   The Jesuits expelled from Spain and the Empire.

1769   Spanish begin the occupation of Upper California.

1774   The Spanish Crown takes over collection of tithes from the church.

1776   Establishment of the Viceroyalty of the Río de la Plata, and the Commandancy General of the Interior Provinces (northern Mexico and the [modern] Southwestern U.S.).

1777   Spanish forces capture Colônia do Sacramento, thus expelling the Portuguese from what became modern Uruguay.

1778   Free Trade Reglamento, permitting unrestricted commerce between nearly all Spanish American ports and the main ports of Spain.

1779   Spain enters the War of the American Revolution on the side of France.

1780   Túpac Amaru rebellion (1780–1783) in Peru.

1781   Comunero Revolt (1781–82) in New Granada.

1783   Treaty of Versailles, by which Spain's recovery of Florida during the war was confirmed.

1787   Society of Friends of the Country (Sociedad de Amigos del País), showing **rising** creole interest in political economy and useful knowledge, established in Havana; a number of others soon established elsewhere in America.

1788   Charles IV (1788–1808).

1793   Spain enters the war against France.

1794   *Consulados,* reflecting expanded commerce in Spanish America, established in Guatemala, Buenos Aires, Cartagena, and Santiago de Chile.

1795   Spain makes peace with France and signs a treaty of alliance (1796); Spain fights on side of France to 1808.

1797   Ships of friendly neutrals permitted to trade direct with Spanish America.

1800   Spain cedes the Louisiana territory to France.

1804   Property belonging to pious works authorized for public sale as a means of raising Crown revenue. The act was considered anti-clerical by Conservatives.

1806–07   Creole militia at Buenos Aires drives the British from the city, which they had captured without authorization by the London government.

1808   Charles IV and his popularly acclaimed successor and son, Ferdinand VII, held prisoners in France as French troops invade Spain. Within two years, virtually the whole country was overrun.

The Conflict of Opinion

PROGRESS

"By this sure but long road [education in the sciences] then, we shall develop our unrivaled local resources, and as a result we shall achieve our own happiness and repay the Crown for showing us how to develop our economy."

— TOMÁS LURQUÍN

"All I have said shows that the Spanish administration was neither indifferent nor antagonistic to the progress of the colony; on the contrary, Spain zealously sought to promote progress and stimulate a general increase of productivity. An unprecedented well-being and prosperity were the fruits of the generous, praiseworthy reforms of which we were the beneficiaries."

— ANGEL CÉSAR RIVAS

"Although the mercantile system has enriched a few persons, it has impoverished and left in misery the rest of the population; it has been a terrible and cruel whip that has lashed the American people."

— MIGUEL RAMOS ARIZPE

LIBERTY

"It is a fact as well known as it is regrettable that the Spanish court has for three long centuries been preoccupied with its own aggrandizement and with that of its governors. Since it was impossible to reconcile this aim with the liberties and economic interests of the people, the result was a terrible conflict of interests. Power and authority conquered; the sacred rights of man were crushed to earth. Out of this conquest rose a system that made government synonymous with despotism, stupidity and vice itself."

— MIGUEL RAMOS ARIZPE

"The creoles, who from the beginning exercised command, who established municipal government, who defended it against absolutism and centralism, were the same colonists that resurrected from oblivion the old supremacy of the cabildos and proclaimed independence. They were essentially Spanish, by race, by tradition, by custom. They were the descendants of the daring and energetic conquistadors who braved unknown seas to conquer a continent; they were the descendants of those who had acquired the precious gem of liberty, of those who in eight centuries had reconquered the fatherland by courage and tenacity, and who laid the basis for the greatest empire in the world."

— ANGEL CÉSAR RIVAS

FAITH

"Religion, resting on eternal foundations, does not fear free discussion. . . . Light is incompatible with darkness; the evangelical maxims are the light. . . . Religion has two kinds of enemies: fanatics and the impious. . . . The impious ridicule religion; the fanatic does what is worse — he makes it detestable. But fanaticism and impiety will pass away. Only religion is eternal."

— VICENTE AZUERO

". . . The Mexican Church ended the eighteenth century and began the following one with both arms broken — the arm of the Inquisition and that of the church-led schools. The head of the church, the episcopacy, was confused; the body of the nation, the aristocracy, was infected by Free-masonry, and afflicted with the cancer of impiety."

— MARIANO CUEVAS, S.J.

"Far from impugning the Catholic faith, [Jeremy] Bentham supports it as indispensable for happiness."

— VICENTE AZUERO

"Like a plant surrounded by nettles, spiritualism will soon die out in a nation that adopts Benthamism as its guide for public education."

— JOSÉ MANUEL GROOT

PROGRESS

The question whether material progress was possible under the Bourbons was not, like faith and liberty, a vital issue in subsequent civil wars in the Spanish-speaking world. But it was long part of patriotic liberal credo in Spanish America that independence was justified by the economic backwardness attendant to the colonial relation with Spain. The selections that follow, however, show diametrically opposite judgments of Bourbon leadership with respect to progress, reflecting a great variance in regional conditions and in the outlook of the writers. The four readings in this first section include two by Mexican priests and one by a Chilean merchant, all of the years immediately before independence, and one by a conservative Venezuelan historian of the twentieth century.

The Delightful Field Ahead

TOMÁS LURQUÍN

Little is known of the merchant, Tomás Lurquín. That he was a wealthy merchant and a Spaniard is likely because of his selection as acting secretary of the *consulado* at Santiago de Chile in 1801. That he possessed a classical education and was well informed of events in Spain is apparent from his address before that body. But what he best represents is that radiantly optimistic faith in material progress and in the capacity of the Bourbons to share it with their entire empire—given peace and time—that characterized the eighteenth-century reformers. Unfortunately, there was to be neither peace nor time, and it may be that Lurquín's faith owed rather too much to that patience with which the well-born have always awaited their Utopias. In the following selection, his address to the Crown is a mere formality; he was actually speaking to local merchants, landowners, and officials.

POLITICAL economy is the science of leading men to happiness, of furnishing them the means of subsistence and of comfort, and of increasing their needs artificially by reason of the facility it has of satisfying their natural needs. It shows them how to produce more, to increase their population and their national strength. This science was formerly unknown; it was created by centuries of experience. In its development, one prejudice often fought with another.

And just as a diamond is cut only by another, so could political economy be shaped only by combating one deeply rooted error with a new one. Man, ever inclined to extremes, at one time gloried in ignorance. At another, he wanted to know everything and rushed beyond his mental limits, reducing all knowledge to rules whose main defect was the little meditation behind their formation and the lack of examination of the circumstances in which they were to

Address of Tomás Lurquín to the *consulado*, Santiago de Chile, Jan 12, 1801, in Miguel Cruchaga Montt, *Obras*, 10 vols. (Madrid, 1929), IV, 281–299. Used by permission of Instituto Editorial Reus.

1

operate. The obstinacy of good intention without informed principles caused man to waste much time off the true path toward knowledge.

Finally, man learned that the general state of happiness was the sum of the happiness of individuals. He learned to pursue this goal slowly, starting with man and human affairs in the most rudimentary situations. He learned that there is no better means to happiness than man himself who can study patiently but zealously the means of aiding Nature; that the goal can best be achieved by men combining their knowledge and efforts with others who are working for the same goal, that he could perform no act more religious than to instruct others in how to achieve happiness. He learned that the best occupation he could engage in was to improve the fortune of the society of which he and other benefactors were members, that there is no better policy than one which increases the population, shapes good character, and creates a vigorous state, that is, one which has a flourishing agriculture, industry, and commerce. This is the reason that patriotic bodies called Academic Societies were formed; this is their objective. Economic societies and *consulados* have been established in Europe and have spread throughout the world with the speed of light, which shines through whatever is placed in its path.

That men should live together follows from human nature and the conditions of life: man's natural ignorance, his needs, his long period of infancy, the marked differences among men in strength, talents, and motives — all these caused men to live in groups to offset their individual weaknesses. Certain elemental truths always existed; they were the possession of but a few minds who tried to extend them to the confused mass of people living in ignorance. The virtue of beneficence, for example, had always been known. It was known that knowledge, and cooperation among peoples, were necessary to make beneficence effective. Philanthropists, wise men, and beneficent societies have existed in all places and

times as evidence of this truth. But the good intentions which motivated these men and societies resulted in little improvement for society. The principles underlying a philosophy of progress had not been discovered; the few unorganized ideas motivating beneficence produced millions of chimerical schemes but little solid accomplishment. To formulate principles was the work of many centuries; its perfection was achieved in the 18th century. With this century of Enlightenment began the happy dynasty of the august Bourbons; they held aloft the Light and diffused it throughout the Empire; the monarch who now occupies the throne [Charles IV] has just extended it to the ends of his dominions; now we are the recipients of his royal beneficence.

Philip V deserved to be called the Brave not only for the courage he demonstrated in opposing the claim to the throne to which his rights, Providence, and his virtues called him; he deserved it for having brought true prosperity to his people in spite of his many problems. He made them aware of the vast resources of the Empire, and he revealed the great mine of talents and wealth that had been buried under an unjust economic system. During his reign the leading statesmen of the nation gathered for the first time to discuss what could be done for the material progress of the whole Empire. Their discussions ranged, so to speak, from the highest concerns of justice, foreign policy, and government, to the simple truths on whose base could be solidly erected the immense edifice of national power and wealth. They began with an interchange of ideas; they continued by studying practical sciences and gathering knowledge from all Europe. They demonstrated the knowledge that aims to bring happiness to humanity and well deserves the name of wisdom. The short but happy reign of Ferdinand VI saw the flourishing of the seeds which barely germinated during the previous one; maritime commerce increased and the country demonstrated that it had even better means than other countries of developing manufacturing.

On succeeding to the throne, Charles III left a kingdom of which he was the conqueror and father to come to a kingdom which Heaven destined to be the object of his unusual beneficence. He brought to it all the knowledge gained in the one he had left enlightened and well developed. He brought with him learned men in many fields of knowledge, but especially those skilled in matters which would assure the material progress of his new vassals. Persuaded that the quest for vainglory to satisfy royal ambition is futile, he aspired only to receive and merit gratitude from his subjects; to accomplish this what could he choose to do more certain of results than protect agriculture, industry, and commerce? Behold, gentlemen, how the wise king blessed our *consulado* and set us on the pathway we now follow. To accomplish these purposes, he populated the desolate Sierra-Morena [mountains of southern Spain], distributed lands that were nominally common but were actually used by no one. The people who needed them most lacked the means of working them. He reduced the privileges of the nobility on the land and permitted grain seeds to be sold free of taxes. He abolished the guild monopolies, and permitted them to continue only as training schools; he bestowed honors on artisans and granted special favors to manufacturing. He established peace in the Mediterranean. He prosecuted vagrancy and established aid for poor workers. He established patriotic societies like this one for the purpose of creating jobs, finding markets, and in general working for the common good. Like a majestic river, which not only irrigates the lands of its source but also reaches remote regions, the king has been placed by Providence at the head of a great monarchy to look after the well-being of the Empire. He has established frequent and regular communications with these dominions; he has broken the chains of commerce; he has drawn closer the ties that unite us; he has opened new markets for the reciprocal trade of both continents.

He would not merit the praise that posterity will bestow upon him if he had employed merely authority and arbitrary means to accomplish his beneficial purposes. The greatest benefits have been discredited by monarchs who forcibly imposed them. The more forcibly the reform is imposed, the less time it endures. King Charles, wiser, chose the way that assures permanence for reforms; he publicized his plans for reform so that the people had time to appreciate the need for them. He prepared the nation for them, infusing into it the spirit on which their success mainly depends. Knowing that palliatives are poor remedies to cure the ills of a state, he rejected the local remedies suggested by various subjects throughout the Empire. Some thought a strong navy was the key to power, others advised government support of agriculture, and still others advised expanding the raising of sheep. Some would even man the galleys with vagrants, expel the *moriscos*,[1] prohibit the importation of foreign manufactures. Others believed the loss of town lands was the cause of decadence. Some thought the cause was the export of precious metals, and others thought inflation caused by precious metals from America was to blame. In short, there was no defect that was not advocated as the only cause of decadence.

But the causes were confused with the effects. Excessive taxes, church lands, and luxury were believed to undermine the common good. Everything was attacked and everything defended but nothing was changed. This piecemeal approach to reform made the carrying out of any one of them very difficult. Symptoms rather than causes were treated. Reforming efforts were weakened by rivalries among officials and plans for reforms often were never executed because of fruitless arguing about theories — the spirit of discord and Aristotelianism that was our unfortunate legacy from the Arabs. Each one formed his own program which he defended vigorously even if it was proved to be utterly unworkable. In this

---

[1] Moors who were forcibly converted in the sixteenth century.

atmosphere even good ideas, advocated by wise and patriotic statesmen, were suffocated by thousands of petty and irrelevant arguments. No one was on the scene who could coordinate the best of these ideas so that some advantage could be derived from the labor expended on many diverse plans for reform.

Our Spain has always produced great men; let there be a need for greatness and great men have risen to fill that need. Poets, warriors, savants, statesmen, theologians — all have risen when circumstances required their talents. They have especially risen to the occasion when asked to do so by the king, as if the king, like the Creator, had only to wish and the thing was done. It was this royal influence that explains how a certain magistrate[2] could astonish the court with the most just, comprehensive, simple, and useful plan for reform imaginable. Having conceived this plan in spite of many other duties engaging his attention, he spoke the truth clearly and vigorously; he swept aside all previous obstacles: private interests, indecision, uncritical love of the past, horror at new truths — all these fled covering their eyes as they ran. He cleansed the horizon of the fatal egoism that had dominated state policies, and substituted for it the public spirit that finds a haven only in great and virtuous souls. His book of gold, *La industria y educación popular*, was read with enthusiasm. The nobility, clergy, merchants — in fact all classes — now had the opportunity to present their ideas; joining in societies, they discussed and revised these ideas and publicized them for the information of the people. In these societies, capital, knowledge, and human effort, which had previously been mysteriously withheld from public benefit, now flowed freely as their members spared nothing to publicize — this became the motto of these beneficent groups. As a result the Empire was enlightened, and since enlightenment necessarily produces prosperity, the nation is on the way toward

2 Pedro Rodríguez, Count of Campomanes (1723–1802).

the place that is occupied today by others who have trod this path rather than the one of destructive warfare.

These benefits had not yet been extended to America; they could not be in the ordinary course of things. What America needed was a means of bringing her enlightened men together, funds to carry out plans with, and other ideas. All at once this best of monarchs provided what was needed by establishing *consulados* such as this one, and we saw what we desired spring up before our eyes. In this institution, the means of reform is united with the power of doing positive good; the means of conquering the Hydra of mercantile disputes is joined with the means of protecting and developing the resources of this kingdom that it might become rich, populous, and happy.

What an enormous, delightful field lies before those who are to cultivate it! Although they are familiar with the field, they must not let their initial enthusiasm be killed by the multitude of small defects that will be brought to their attention. Since they cannot possibly deal with all of them at once, they must use discernment and judgment in determining the priority of their tasks.

The reforms began with the parts of the economy under crown control. The first obstacle removed was the inveterate law suits over the *alcabala* [excise tax], which were endless, and the fees by which pettifoggers made a living from them. One can appreciate what this reform meant only by leafing through the books I have here before me. Hundreds of verbal complaints and hundreds of formal suits have been concluded within five years without undue expense or trouble for the litigants. This is unquestionable proof of the importance and the competence of this *consulado*.

From the beginning, it was appreciated that the country could not be developed unless there were men who knew how to increase production and improve its quality, to create new occupations, and to direct reforms. These men must be educated in the principles of national development. The European people were convinced that the empirical methods of the past bound them to a narrow circle of thought incapable of producing change or coping with present problems. They eagerly embraced the useful sciences. They were also persuaded that because knowledge of these sciences would permit man to discover the innermost secrets of nature, would free skilled hands for labor, and would lift the veil of ignorance, education must include these sciences. Natural history, physics, metallurgy, calculus, the principles of commerce and industry, mineralogy, and economy — all these would open the doors to national development. By this sure but long road, then, we shall develop our unrivaled local resources, and as a result we shall achieve our own happiness and repay the crown for showing us how to develop our economy. We need only a professor of chemistry to complete our university staff; when the war is over, we shall receive other benefits such as financial aid to students proficient in these sciences that make man truthful, sincere, modest, and industrious.

But the *consulado* has accomplished some lesser things while waiting for these important benefits. A small class, whose members are to become teachers, has been trained in certain of the useful arts. They can teach unskilled persons, who are the ones most in need of work. Training will be given in the production of those items that are susceptible of wide development in this country, and are needed in Spain to free her from dependence on rival nations. These will be products suitable to our climate and capable of giving permanent employment to the greatest number of people. These people are now unemployed, having been forced into an idleness that is the cause for vice and misery and an alarming decrease in the population. As a result of the cultivation of these new products, a new class of consumers will have been created, and there will be a lessening of the languor, spirit of dejection, and laziness that has been man's inveterate attitude. These new

industries will not increase, fortunately, the number of people who are satisfied with the bare essentials of existence. As a first step, a trial has been made with flax, which has been planted, harvested, and sent to the textile factories of Spain. There this flax has found a market that was doubtless extraordinary; we are presently, however, cut off from the latest news. We have sent to Spain a list of products suitable to our warm spring weather and have asked which of them would have a market there; as soon as we have received a reply, experiments will be made to determine which of those in demand grow well. The most suitable products will then be given a protected market in Spain, and their production here will be greatly increased.

Although the improvement of roads has not been specifically entrusted to the *consulado*, this *junta* has always regarded it as necessary for the increase of trade. This *junta* gathered all the information available about the road over the *cordillera*, which has always been considered shorter than the one being used; following this, a survey of the road was made. Inevitably, accidents occurred during this survey that made impossible an objective consideration of the advantages of this new route. The zealous and industrious citizen who promised to undertake this survey was old and in poor health; his efforts caused his death. Time does not permit me to praise him in the terms of gratitude that we all feel; I can only say he will be remembered with the greatest esteem for his praiseworthy intentions. The professor who accompanied him has also died. With both men gone, the work had to be suspended till some happy day in the future.

The *junta* has also been concerned with building a dock at the main port of the kingdom that will eliminate the present hard labor of loading and unloading produce into small boats. The work has not yet been started because members have been unable to agree on a plan. But because of its importance, all the obstacles that presently make the horrible route around Cape

Horn preferable to this route will be swept away and the regions along this interior road will benefit from this commerce.

*   *   *

But to enumerate all matters this *junta* has been involved in would try Your Excellency's patience. I can assure you that there are few matters it has not been concerned with. All who wish to examine the record of transactions are invited to do so. They will find the truth of this statement in the record. In examining these transactions they will also learn not only how these matters have been conducted but will see evidence of the tireless zeal that has motivated this body. They will see in these papers a harmony of ideas, a constant concern for improvement, and the spirit of cooperativeness in which all men of good will and of public spirit have united their efforts. It is true that excellent rules of government have contributed to the happiness, organization, and progress of the *consulado*. These rules have remained unaltered since they were sent from Spain. All those taking part have done so with the aim of realizing the high purposes of the sovereign. Our *consulado* has not been inflicted with the terrible disease that has claimed certain others — the mania of arrogating oneself over others, of championing only private and narrow interests, and especially of raising objections to whatever is suggested with a kind of stupid pride in being argumentative. Such practices would have made the provisions of the king useless if not actually harmful. This *consulado* has from the outset silenced defenses of misery and ignorance on the grounds that local customs and practices cannot be altered. We have believed in the ideas of certain outstanding men; we have let ourselves be led by their wise hands; we have followed their light. Under this principle, the *consulado* has accepted patriotism and truth as its polestar. It has consistently followed the leadership of the officers who have been in charge since its establishment. Thus I run no risk of being mistaken when I predict that we are secure from the ruinous mania of disapproving what has been accomplished simply because we ourselves did not do it. This attitude is a terrible sickness because it can prevent the greatest undertaking; worse, it can even prevent remedies for existing ills.

Unconcerned with either exaggerated praise or vituperative criticism, the *consulado* will calmly continue along the road it has laid out that will lead the people to prosperity. But it will not disdain suggestions made by the public. It will adopt some and reject others, having in mind always only the public happiness.

A just government looks upon our labors with pleasure. Although we may not always be successful, we shall always be perseverant and guided by the sublime maxim that by right intentions and judicious means all things are possible.

Prosperity — the Fruit of Generous Reforms

ANGEL CÉSAR RIVAS

Angel César Rivas (?–1930), was born in Sucre State, Venezuela. He was graduated from Central University of Venezuela with a doctorate in political science and was later professor of government and international law at that institution. Widely traveled, he conducted research in the archives of the United States and Europe for his writings, which include *Origins of the Independence of Venezuela** (1909), his published discourse on initiation into the National Academy of History; *The Second Mission to Spain of Don Fermín Toro* (1907); and *Essays of Political and Diplomatic History* (1916). The following selection is taken from the last-named work.

PHILIP V and his successors, inspired by the ideas and the scientific knowledge that was part of the eighteenth-century European cultural environment, began at once to devote some of their governmental activity to the material development of Venezuela, and to furnish our region the means of achieving the prosperity made possible by our fertile soil and geographical situation. It was also at this time that the Bourbons, without being aware of it, supplied Venezuela with what Becerra[1] has accurately called "the contribution of Spain toward the dethronement of its own monarchs."

The important fact about the progress of Venezuela in the eighteenth century is the concession to commerce that Philip V made in 1728 to the Guipúzcoa [Caracas] Company. The measures taken in 1717, 1718, and 1720 prohibiting the importation into Spain of American products brought directly by foreigners, and reducing the taxes on cacao had not had the desired effect. From 1722 to 1728 only five Spanish ships

arrived at Spain with cacao from Venezuela, even though the price of cacao had risen in Spain to eighty pesos a bushel during these years. In the colony, on the other hand, imports continued to be supplied by the Dutch from Curaçao; this fact alone kept the commerce with Spain limited to a negligible volume.

In accordance with the *cedula* of September 25, 1728, the company was given privileges including the right to trade with Venezuela; it was to drive contraband trade from the coasts and to apprehend those involved in it. The company did not begin operations till 1730 when the first commercial voyage was made to Venezuela by its vessels. The influence of the Dutch was so strong, and the hatred for the company by those who traded with the Dutch so great, that the company experienced great difficulties in getting established. Only after two years was the company able to attract enough cacao to load one of the four merchant ships that made up the 1730 expedition.

The company, which was organized with a fleet of twelve ships whose purpose was to drive out contraband, also built warehouses

*This and other Spanish titles have been translated by the editor.

[1] Ricardo A. Becerra (1836–1905), Venezuelan historian.

From Angel César Rivas, *Ensayos de Historia y Política y Diplomática* (Madrid, 1916), pp. 68–77, 90–96.

and other storage facilities that can still be seen in La Guaira, Puerto Cabello, and other places. Because of the company's mercantile activities, Puerto Cabello became a city with many fine homes and with large buildings to serve the needs of commerce; it furnished capital by which the production of cacao and other products were much increased. The company imported from Spain goods in sufficient quantities to meet the needs of the colonists. The considerable increase in commerce that the company achieved, its beneficial influence for agriculture, its development of several towns, the increase of royal income, the importation and circulation of capital, and the financial aid rendered the Crown by the company in the war against England in 1740, all explained the grant to them in 1742 of a mercantile monopoly of Venezuela. This was extended in 1752 to include Maracaibo.

To evaluate the benefit to the colony and the influence on its development that was due to the company, it is perhaps fitting to cite the dispassionate comments of Bello:[2]

Whatever the abuses of its privileges may have been that turned the country against the company, it cannot be denied that the company gave movement to the machine the conquest had established and evangelical zeal had organized. The conquerors and the conquered, united by one language and one faith into a single family, saw the land prosper that was irrigated by their sweat. They and their mother country could now reap the benefits rather than the Dutch monopoly. It was not only the cultivation of cacao that laid the basis for agriculture in the excellent soil of Venezuela. New products were introduced that added greatly to a rising agricultural prosperity. The Aragua valley[3] underwent an economic recovery with the crops introduced by Biscayans; the development was greatly aided by the industrious habits of Canary Islanders. The cultivation and manufacture of indigo was hardly known before in these valleys; now with this and other products, there was an

increase of wealth and of population that could hardly have been surpassed in any other area. From La Victoria [Aragua valley] to Valencia, happiness and abundance were the main characteristics of life.

It required only a few years under the stimulative labor of the Biscayans to transform the colony to a prosperous one and to supply the means for a continuing increase of agricultural wealth. Although the monopoly was justified in the beginning in order that the company might supply the colony what was needed to give value to the land and guarantee the company a return on its capital, later, when colonists desired to start new industries, the monopoly was regarded as an insupportable tyranny.

That the important and salutary change taking place in Venezuela and Maracaibo in the course of a few years was mainly due to the Biscayans can easily be demonstrated. That change was registered in the exports made by the company, in the immigration it encouraged, in the idle land it brought into production, and in the new crops it introduced. The most important change of all, however, was an indirect effect of the economic development: the energy displayed by all classes of society, especially by the middle class, in attempting to end the monopoly. The company came to be regarded as tyrannical because it gradually gained control of all agriculture and commerce in the colony; it even became an influential adviser of the administration and the government. If the *cabildo* and the leading citizens of Caracas had not displayed a conduct that was somewhat fainthearted and tinged with political opportunism, the movement of protest led by [Juan Francisco de] León would have ended the privileges of the company and established a regime of commercial liberties like that Charles III gave to the Americans years later.

The company successfully repelled the rude assault that the motley followers of León tried to launch against it. Their privileges, nonetheless, were not left entirely

[2] Andrés Bello (1781–1865), Venezuelan poet and scholar.
[3] A fertile region southwest of Caracas.

untouched. For some time thereafter the victory of the company and the defeat of the *cabildo* [city council] seemed permanent. The company had powerful friends in the court at Madrid; in Venezuela, the predominant effect of the House of Bourbon was to centralize power, to exercise vigilance in order to prevent any further uprising, and to curtail the power of the *cabildo*. But the clamor of the Venezuelans did not forever fall on deaf ears. In less than ten years after the revolt against the company, doubtless for the purposes of submitting the company to closer control and placating the Venezuelans who had continued to file complaints against it, a royal ordinance of 1751 transferred the direction of the company from San Sebastián to Madrid. Later, in 1759, the Court ordered that one sixth of the cargo space of each merchant vessel of the company be reserved for agricultural producers and merchants, who could ship cacao to Spain on their own accounts. They were guaranteed a price by the Crown of sixteen pesos[4] a bushel for cacao instead of the ten pesos they had been receiving. They were also granted a price of thirteen reales a pound for indigo, which was three reales higher than they had received from the company. Under this double blow, justly and prudently aimed at their privileges, the company began to decline at a time when the future of the colony began to appear brighter. Because of the influence of a former governor of Venezuela, then serving on His Majesty's Council, a law in 1752 provided for an increase in the number of shareholders, part of whom were to be Caraqueños and other inhabitants of the country. There followed, in 1765, the decree of Charles III opening the commerce of Margarita and Trinidad to all his subjects. In 1774 a royal *cedula* was published that permitted New Spain, Guatemala, New Granada and Peru to trade freely with each other. Finally, in 1776, this monarch completely ended Crown participation in

merchant shipping and authorized the establishment of both foreign and Spanish private commercial companies. The monopoly of the company was now practically extinguished; not until February 15, 1781, however, did a royal *cedula* officially abolish its privileges. The company then broke up into several small private firms.

Whatever may have been the bad effects caused by the company, the greatest of them was doubtless the paralysis of the economic development of the colony. One cannot deny, however, that the level of wealth in the country differed greatly after the period of company development from what it was in 1730. On the average, the company exported annually in its later years, 36,000 bushels of cacao, 225,000 pounds of indigo, and 15,000 cowhides; its exports went not only to Spain but to Mexico and to the Canary Islands. It is worthy of note that up to 1763, there had been legally exported from Venezuela, 80,000 bushels of cacao, 325,000 pounds of tobacco, and 35,000 cowhides. In addition to an increase in the production of agriculture and livestock, the company opened roads, founded towns and cities, created new industries such as shipbuilding, and because of a continuous stream of immigration that the company encouraged, the population was increased by immigrants from Northern Spain. Mixing their blood with the descendants of the early colonists, these Basques and Navarrese proved to be of great value to the country. Most of them engaged in agriculture or some other industry; when the time for independence arrived, they did their part to win it. As a result of the economic development generated by the company, it was now possible to meet not only the expenses of the government but to provide capital for further development. This need had been fully met only by a subsidy from Mexico. This transformation brought about by the company also made possible, shortly before its abolition, the establishment of an intendancy by which the financial administration of the colony was organized and made uniform under the Ordinances for Intendants in

[4] Standard coin in the colonies, which was worth 8 reales.

effect in New Spain and Buenos Aires. Thus when we weigh the good and bad results of this commercial company, we may gladly accept the opinion of Andrés Bello. He attributed to the Guipúzcoa Company both the economic progress and the hindrances to that progress that alternated in the political regeneration of Venezuela.

Although the company did not succeed in extending its monopoly over Nueva Andalucía and Guayana [both in Eastern Venezuela], the condition of these two provinces was also improved during the time of the company. In Nueva Andalucía, there were by this time four or five times as many towns as there had been at the end of the seventeenth century; its inhabitants, without particular protection by the Crown, engaged in agriculture, fishing, livestock raising, and commerce. In the region of the Guianese missions, the Capuchins had during these years more than twenty-five Indian towns, and large herds of cattle and horses. The Franciscans, together with the governors, especially the intelligent and vigorous Centurión, were successful in re-occupying for the mother country the territory that the Dutch had long held. The economic progress was enough for the governor just mentioned, who was the first to comprehend that the future colonization of Guiana depended on a civil government in place of government by the regular clergy, to give an unusual direction to the development of the province. He organized exploring expeditions toward Parima,[5] found ways to expel the Dutch permanently, and founded towns and other settlements.

*   *   *

The regulation of free commerce permitted the ports of Venezuela — both large and small ones — to trade directly with all the ports of Spain that were permitted to trade with America. Under these conditions the colonists could devote themselves to agriculture and livestock-raising with confidence that their produce had a market overseas. There were some products, how-

ever, that could not be easily shipped to Spain. A very enlightened intendant, Francisco Saavedra, took account of this fact in 1784 when he granted permission to Venezuelans to trade with neighboring foreign colonies. Only cacao was excepted from this trade. They were permitted to import from these colonies agricultural machinery, slaves, and gold and silver. The colonists derived great benefits from this decree, which meant a radical change in the mercantile system of the times. About 10,000 mules, which sold at twenty-five pesos a head and up, were annually shipped from Coro, Puerto Cabello, Barcelona, Cumaná, Guarapiche, and Angostura. This shipping, which included certain other colonial products, was valued at about 2,500,000 bolívars [pesos] a year, and brought much needed coin into the country.

The treaty of alliance with the French Republic, which Spain signed on August 18, 1796, obligated the latter to engage in open warfare with England. To do so was the equivalent for Spain of depriving herself of direct commerce with her colonies and abandoning them to trade with friendly neutrals. Since the high seas were soon thereafter controlled by the English navy and English corsairs, the king opened the Indies to neutral trade by a *cedula* of November 18, 1797. Under this new provision, neutral ships could trade with the colonies either from Spain or direct from their home ports and could carry either Spanish or foreign goods. Almost at once ships from many foreign nations called at the ports of Venezuela; new markets were thus established, new contracts made, and economic development underwent another upsurge. A region like Cumaná, which before 1793 saw no more than two or three Spanish ships a year, became by the early years of the nineteenth century a thriving mercantile center. Barcelona, which had annually exported in 1761 only 6,000–8,000 cattle, sold during the Truce of Amiens [1802–03], 132,000 cattle, 2,100 horses, 84,000 mules, 800 donkeys, 18 million pounds of jerked beef, 36,000 cowhides, and 6,000 deer hides. Guayana, which at mid-century

[5] Sierra Parima, which forms part of the boundary with Brazil.

had only one town — the *presidio* of Santo Tomé — and had about 1,800 head of cattle, was exporting cattle by the end of the century. Its great river, previously visited clandestinely by the Dutch, saw in only four months in 1782 thirty-two merchant ships. The missions of the Orinoco where the priests had established a cattle industry and which had had only 14,000 to 16,000 head during the time of Diguja's *visita,* now had more than 180,000 head of cattle.

The increase in production that followed the passing of the Reglamento of Free Commerce was of such magnitude that in 1796, a year before opening the colonial ports to foreign commerce, the imports of Venezuela amounted to 3,115,811 pesos; the exports in 1780, at the end of the monopoly of the Guipúzcoa Company, amounted to two million pesos; they amounted to 3,139,-682 pesos in 1796. The measure passed in 1797, cited earlier, naturally gave the colonies a larger vision of their commercial possibilities. In the years to 1810, the value of exports rose to 4,776,500 pesos, a figure which excludes any estimate of the value of contraband trade. Dauxion,[6] who had the opportunity of examining the archives of the neighboring colonies, estimated the value of exports from Venezuela during these years at 5,200,000 pesos.

This increase in production was accompanied by the spread of agriculture and livestock raising into new regions. Regions like Guayana, and Nueva Andalucía, among others, all of which had been undeveloped until then, were drawn into the economic development initiated earlier to the west. But the transformation of these provinces was necessarily limited as they enjoyed only a few years of progress before 1810. Bello refers to this:

The eastern part of the province was engaged in raising cotton, which strongly contributed to the rise of Venezuelan commerce. The cattle from the *llanos* became a source of wealth as they could now be exported from Barcelona and Coro, and Guayana found a new industry in the cultivation of tobacco at

Barinas that found preference over many other tobaccos in Venezuela and on the European markets.

The great upsurge in agricultural production and trade could not have been so notable had it not been for an increase in population. A large number of planters and merchants from Spain and the Canary Islands entered the country after the Free Trade Reglamento was enacted; beyond this, the authorities openly welcomed the French colonists who at a later time fled from Martinique and Guadaloupe, and the Spanish inhabitants of Trinidad who fled from that island in 1797 on the British occupation. Along the whole coast of the Gulf of Paria [between Trinidad and the mainland], new towns sprang up as a result of this immigration. The immigrants came to stay, and took up permanent residence with their slaves in these towns. When Dauxion visited this coast in 1807, he estimated a population of 7,000 persons among whom, in Dauxion's words, "were some men who had lived in the most brilliant social circles of Germany and France."

We can estimate the population of Venezuela at this time from various sources. Caracas, which in 1696 had only 6,000 inhabitants, was a city of 47,000 in 1810. The population of Cumaná and Barcelona in 1761 was 4,372 and 3,351 persons, respectively; by 1810, these towns counted 28,000 and 14,000 persons. . . . On the basis of Humboldt's calculations, we can say that the total population of the Captaincy General was 900,000 persons at the beginning of the 19th century. By 1810, it would not be out of line to assume a figure of 1,000,000 persons. Of these, some 200,000 were white.

All I have said shows that the Spanish administration was neither indifferent nor antagonistic to the progress of the colony; on the contrary, Spain zealously sought to promote progress and stimulate a general increase of productivity. An unprecedented well-being and prosperity were the fruits of the generous praiseworthy reforms of which we were the beneficiaries.

[6] Jean Francois Dauxion-Lavaysse (1775–1826).

Monopoly and Misery

MIGUEL RAMOS ARIZPE

Born near Saltillo, Coahuila, Miguel Ramos Arizpe (1775–1843) was educated for the priesthood, taking orders in Mexico City in 1803. He received a doctorate in canon law in 1807 from the University of Guadalajara and three years later received a doctorate in civil law from the College of Law in the capital. Aware of how little his own region had benefited from the Bourbon reforms, he was well suited by education, outlook, and domestic travels to represent the Interior Provinces of the Oriente (Coahuila, Nuevo León, Tamaulipas, and Texas) at the *Cortes* of Cádiz. There he delivered in 1812 a memorial which expressed his dream of liberty and progress for the Northeast. Imprisoned during the reaction in Spain (1814–1820), he was released in time to return to Mexico to take part in the independence movement of 1821. He was an author of the Constitution of 1824 and served until his death in various civil and ecclesiastical positions. The selection that follows is taken from his memorial to the *Cortes*.

PUBLIC EDUCATION

THE support of public education is one of the primary obligations of all enlightened governments; only despots and tyrants support ignorance to make easier the violation of individual rights and liberties. The isolation of the four Internal Provinces of Oriente, the character of their local governments, and the notorious slowness of the monarchical government, are all responsible for the absence in these miserable provinces of a single, regularly established, public school. A primary school teacher receives a small, regular salary only in Saltillo, the most important villa of the province of Coahuila, and in Monterrey, the capital of the kingdom of Nuevo León. From [militia] company funds and private contributions, the *presidios* and *villas* with larger population support some inept so-called teachers who teach the Christian doctrine poorly; generally, they are incapable of instructing even in the fundamentals of a regular primary education. Ordinarily, there is a little school or two on the *haciendas* where many people live and work. But I have often observed that the *hacendados* prevent their workers' sons from learning to write; they fear that a little education would enlighten them, and they would then reject the harsh servitude of their parents and seek a less miserable way of life. Unhappy American youth! Can it be possible they intend to repress the finest tendencies of your nature in order to keep you ignorant and hence enslaved?

*　　*　　*

I have described the pitiable — even shameful — state of public education in the Interior Provinces. What else could there have been under the kind of government, say, rather, lack of government, that has prevailed? It would be enough for Your Majesty to adopt reforms like those I have described to realize marked improvement in

From Miguel Ramos Arizpe, *Discursos, Memorias e Informes* (Mexico, 1942), pp. 43–54. Used by permission of the Universidad Nacional Autónoma de México. In some instances the excerpts have been rearranged from their order of appearance in the published work.

a matter of great importance to an enlightened government. It is to be hoped that the Superior Junta, the deputations of the provinces, the municipalities, and even the *consulado* will support in every way possible the establishment of schools and public academies for the education and enlightenment of these people. In this way, the foundation will be laid for general happiness. The bishop of this vast diocese will doubtless cooperate in a matter that involves his interests, and Your Majesty will, as soon as possible, establish a general system of public education capable of elevating Spanish American youth to the degree of intellectual brilliance that springs from greatness of character. For these reasons I would ask that Your Majesty establish a Royal University at Linares, Nuevo León, which could be united with the seminary college there until such time as funds are collected permitting its establishment in a separate building. The regulations of the university should be modeled on those of the university at Guadalajara, and the corporation and individuals of the university should enjoy the same rights and privileges that are enjoyed there. A royal college should also be established in Saltillo. This *villa* has 13,000 people not counting the nearby town of San Esteban; it has a healthy climate, a well-developed agriculture and a manufacturing industry, and a building next to the church of San Juan Nepomuceno that can be used for establishment of the college. The government should not consider whether there is sufficient funds for it. Granting the right to establish the college, the populace that has always wanted education will make whatever sacrifice is necessary to obviate the need of sending their sons to Mexico and Guadalajara where they remain because there are no institutions in the Interior Provinces for their suitable employment.

*   *   *

AGRICULTURE

The valuable branch of agriculture, worthy occupation of man, school of a thousand civic virtues, main basis of happiness, and the soundest wealth of the State, ought to be flourishing in these fertile provinces. Their healthy, invigorating climate, their capacity for varied production, their abundant water — all invite man to cultivate the soil. Because of these natural advantages, and in spite of civil war, agriculture is making some progress in the province of Texas, and notably in the provinces of Coahuila and Nuevo León. Unfortunately, the only important agricultural products in Texas are corn, wheat, and sugarcane, which are raised between San Antonio and the Gulf. The main products in Coahuila are corn, wheat, grapes, cotton, beans, pimentos, all kinds of fruit, and abundant and tender vegetables. Corn, which is the main food of the people, yields 100 bushels from a bushel of seed on the poorest lands; on the average, the yield is from 200 to 300 bushels. In Parras, Monclova, and Saltillo, wheat grows abundantly and is of excellent quality. Wheat surplus to the needs of Coahuila is sent to Nuevo León, Nuevo Santander, Texas, and south as far as the mining districts of San Luis Potosí and Zacatecas.

Notwithstanding the restrictions on planting vineyards, they are one of the most profitable crops of these provinces owing to the suitable climate and soil. The vineyards of Cuatrociénegas and Sardinas in San Buenaventura [eastern Coahuila] compare favorably with those of Castile in the length of life of the vine and in the quality and abundance of the grapes. For table wine, Spaniards prefer that from Palomas, near Saltillo, to the best wine of Europe. The greater part of the 10,000 inhabitants in Parras, located in a fertile region, cultivate vineyards; their excellent brandies and full bodied wines are sold in the capital and other places of the kingdom. Unhappy people of Parras, how much opulence would you enjoy today were it not for the greed of the monopolists and the cupidity of the two landlords who bind the arms of your industrious sons? Now dry those tears born of misery while living in a land of abundance. Rest assured that the wise and paternal government will break the fetters of the agricultural monopoly, by permitting you to use the abundant waters granted by Nature, to expand your luxuriant vineyards, and to cause them to resprout and bear fruit abundantly.

* * *

MANUFACTURING

A wise government profits greatly when Nature favors agriculture and livestock-raising, the source of man's happiness, so liberally that they thrive because of Her alone. All the government needs to do is aid them indirectly by the support of manufacturing. Your Majesty now knows of the beneficial influences of Nature and man on agriculture and livestock raising; but I have failed if I do not point out that manufacturing has been incomprehensibly abandoned. I do so confident that I can persuade Your Majesty to protect and develop it. The important cotton manufacturing industry is in such a state of decadence that Coahuila, where cotton grows abundantly, sacrifices all its profit to the provinces to the south. From these manufacturing provinces, where the planters of Coahuila send raw cotton, is received high-priced cloth that has borne the expense of a round trip of more than 800 miles, three or four *alcabalas* (excise taxes), the wages of factory workers, and the profits of middlemen. The women of Coahuila, whose domestic skills can hardly be exaggerated, can scarcely furnish any balance for this uneven exchange. With crude looms that ought to shame an enlightened government, they spin thread and make small items like napkins, towels, and tablecloths; some of these they fashion so well that a tablecloth or a scarf that cost eight pesos to make will sell for forty-five pesos. As an additional means of offsetting our disadvantageous situation, a cotton-manufacturing industry has been started in Saltillo with more than forty looms for weaving coarse cloth. The workers would be in even a better position if they were not obliged to sell their products each week in order to buy cotton for the week following.

Wool, which is clipped twice yearly, is also sent south from where it is returned to Coahuila in the form of hats and blankets and cloth of baize and serge. Owing to the same expenses pertaining to cotton, wool products are sold for seventy-five percent more than if the same product were made locally. Apparently it is the fate of these Spaniards of Coahuila to be the slaves of four greedy merchants in San Luis Potosí and Querétaro. Recently, as a means of relief, a wool-manufacturing industry was established in Saltillo and Tlaxcala, an adjacent pueblo; some sixty looms weave blankets, serge, and coarse frieze. There are also some hat factories that produce low-to-average-grade products. Although there is some iron and wood manufacturing in Saltillo, Parras, and Monterrey, it is a shameful fact that our agricultural tools are still made in Puebla, Mexico City, and San Miguel.

COMMERCE

A province approaches prosperity to the extent that its exports exceed its consumption of any given item. But when its exports are raw materials necessary for its own subsistence, the province, far from being in a state of increasing opulence, is in a state of slavery that probably heralds complete decadence. What good is it for the hungry to have flour if it costs more than the flour is worth to make bread? This is the state of affairs in the provinces of Oriente. There is an abundance of raw materials; but to derive any benefit from them, they must be exported and returned as manufactures at a price four times the cost of the raw materials. Fine wool, excellent cotton, furs, livestock — all products of the sweat of these people — become instruments of their slavery and misery. One year they sell a sheep for twelve reales, a buck goat for eight, and a bull for five pesos; the next year they pay twelve reales for only the wool of that sheep, twelve reales for the buck's hide in the form of Cordovan, and six pesos for the leather from the bull's hide. In this way, the manufacturers and merchants outside the province receive as much or more than they paid for the livestock of these provinces by the sale of only the hides and wool. This condition of slavery of these miserable Spaniards, furthermore, is aggravated by the pernicious and disgraceful monopoly of European imports held in Veracruz and Mexico City.

This, Señor, is the miserable state of commerce of these fertile provinces. This is not, in my opinion, a state of merely passive trade. Rather it is a state of horrible and barbarous servitude. Saltillo, located in the only gap of the Sierra Madre del Oriente range, is the theatre for this scandalous drama. Every year in September, the inhabitants attend the Saltillo fair where they pay tribute to their miserable slavery by parting with their produce for ten pesos only to find they need twenty pesos to clothe themselves. Thus they are obliged to accept goods on credit for which they mortgage their products of the next year. Their debt, a symbol of perpetual slavery, remains year after year; frequently an honest planter or livestock raiser, unable to meet his debt, suffers ruin at one blow — the loss of his small property.

INCREASE OF THE POPULATION

In the Interior Provinces of the Oriente, Your Majesty would be forever gratefully remembered if, in response to the respectful and just pleas of the people, he would put into effect the reforms mentioned. Only by these reforms can the worthy Spanish inhabitants be restored to the state of free men, a state they should always have enjoyed. But a wise and enlightened government does not limit itself to placing the individuals of society in such a state. Knowing the secret springs of the heart, a wise government paves the road to prosperity either by furnishing the means to travel toward it, or by inspiring the populace to overcome any obstacle barring the way. Since Your Majesty is thoroughly imbued with these wise principles of government, I need only call your sovereign attention to the Interior Provinces and make known the easy and effective means by which they can achieve a high degree of prosperity. Their size, climate, produce, and excellent seaports invite millions of men to become rich. But the government has never carried out an effective means of bringing immigrants here; this idea has never progressed beyond mere plans like the one in 1805 that dealt with bringing 6,000 married men to Texas. Perhaps the importance of a project like this is not fully appreciated even by the potential immigrants who might become rich and prosperous. Notwithstanding the present circumstances of the nation, I strongly recommend this project to Your Majesty. The project will profit all who take part in it, will benefit the province of Texas, which needs industrious people, and will add to the security of that important province. In this way, Your Majesty will pave the main road to national prosperity and will extend that of the interior provinces. This road is the increase of population.

FREE COMMERCE AND IMPROVEMENT OF THE PORTS OF THE BAY OF SAN BERNARDO, BRAZO DE SANTIAGO, ETC.

Although the mercantile system has enriched a few persons, it has impoverished and left in misery the rest of the population; it has been a terrible and cruel whip that has lashed the American people. Veracruz is the only free port for the entire kingdom of New Spain and the vast region of the Internal Provinces; in that port all the goods from Europe are controlled by a monopoly. Spanish merchants buy these goods in Cádiz from foreigners. They are resold in Veracruz, and successively in Mexico City, Querétaro, Zacatecas, and at the fair in Saltillo. Finally, after being transported some 2,000 miles from Veracruz, they are sold in the other towns of the Interior Provinces. An *alcabala* has been collected on each sale beginning at Cádiz and ending in the towns of the Interior Provinces. Its collection is inexorable; the poor farmers must pay this tax in Saltillo even if it means parting with the little rice or flour or chickpeas they have reserved for their own food. Moreover, these goods must bear the expense of long transportation by sea and land. All merchants profit — the foreign merchants, those of Cádiz, of Veracruz, of Mexico City, of Saltillo, and even those of the small towns of the Interior Provinces. Only the miserable consumers of the Interior Provinces suffer the burden of all these profits, taxes, and expenses of transportation. Can any of these provinces benefit from a chain of commerce made of such cruel links? All the King's subjects obey the same law and have the same mother; all, in fact, are brothers. Why is there not, then, an equal sharing of rights and obligations? Free commerce is permitted between the ports of Spain and many ports of America. But New Spain has only the funnel of Veracruz. Tampico, Altamira, Soto La Marina, Brazo de Santiago, San Bernardo and other ports, all better than Veracruz, cannot even trade with Havana much less with the ports of Spain. Since most of these ports are in the Interior Provinces, how unjust it is for the people to pay the extra cost for goods from Veracruz, when they might have been sent from Spain or the Caribbean Islands direct to their doorsteps? And if Spanish merchants are permitted to call at the ports of our allies or of neutral countries, why deprive the Spanish Americans of the same privilege? Your Majesty is commendably concerned with this serious matter; on his decision, the permanent union of Spain and the Americas, a question of more than domestic interest, mainly depends. I will defer other matters that I believe are conducive to the happiness of the Interior Provinces and to that of the nation; but I must say to Your Majesty that since freedom from want lies deeply in the heart of every man, the populace of the Interior Provinces will not remain peaceful in the misery and deprivation attendant to a terrible mercantile servitude. Nor will they ever be a prosperous part of the nation till they are granted direct, free commerce so that they may benefit from their own natural wealth. And even when

this is granted, the ports of this coast must be free from taxes, at least temporarily, in order to attract the maximum number of merchants. Although the port of San Bernardo was opened to trade in 1805, few ships have called there. The port should be free from taxes for ten years so that producers and buyers may be attracted to what is now a sparsely populated region. The port of Brazo de Santiago has many natural advantages. The harbor has thirteen feet of water and is protected by islands; the port is located where the provinces of Nuevo Santander, Texas, Coahuila, and Nuevo León converge. The river is navigable for 160 miles and without much labor could be made navigable eighty miles farther. This would reduce the cost of tranportation to inland points, as compared with that from Veracruz, by three fourths. Since the port of Soto la Marina is located at the center of the coast of Nuevo Santander all its 60,000 inhabitants would benefit if it were opened to free commerce. Although sand drifts into its harbor from nearby lakes, this condition could be prevented by a jetty. Altamira, farthest south of the province and thirty-six miles from Tampico, is located at the mouth of the Pánuco and Horcasitas rivers; these are navigable for at least eighty miles. Ships should be given free choice of calling at either Altamira or Tampico since they are separated by navigable lakes.

Your Majesty should not delay the granting of these privileges on the grounds that there are not, as in Spain, towns at the ports. Rather, the establishment of towns on this coast should be prohibited because of the unhealthy climate; it would be enough to build some large warehouses and a shipping office. One need only recall that millions of persons have died in Veracruz to appreciate why towns should not be established. Why is pestilence unknown in Altamira, Soto la Marina, and El Refugio at the mouth of the Brazo de Santiago? Because these towns are some thirty miles from the hot, humid coast.

Granting liberty of commerce to these ports, persons from outside the region will be attracted to the nearby towns; they will guarantee security of the ports because they have a direct interest in them.

Finally, if the commerce of these provinces is to be fully developed, four annual fairs should be established in which goods are sold tax-free for fifteen days. These should be located at Saltillo, where there is presently a fair of limited commerce; at San Antonio in the province of Texas; at Revilla near the mouth of the Rio Grande; and at Padilla in southern Nuevo Santander, where goods may be sent from Soto la Marina and Altamira.

When Your Majesty and the Spanish Government have granted all this, they can be assured of the loyalty of the populace, and can expect blessings from Heaven and from the Americans who will have seen evidence of justice and paternal love, and who will not only reject suggestions of rebellion from foreigners and disloyal subjects, but will shed their blood to preserve the union with the mother country.

The Forgotten Masses

MANUEL ABAD Y QUEIPO

Manuel Abad y Queipo (1751–1825), born in Oviedo, Asturias, and educated for the priesthood, first served in America in Honduras from 1779–84. Transferred to the bishopric of Michoacán, he performed various duties as assistant to the bishop. These duties obliged him to travel extensively among the many Indian pueblos and helped to awaken in him a social conscience fully a century before concern with the lower classes was general in Latin America. He was finally appointed bishop of Michoacán in 1810, but the subsequent rebellions and plots against Spain disrupted his duties and pained his sense of loyalty. An avid reformer but not a revolutionist, he departed for Spain in 1814 and never returned to Spanish America. He was the author of many petitions, pastoral letters and memorials to the Crown and other documents. From one of them, addressed to the Crown in 1799, the following selection is taken.

WE HAVE previously said that New Spain has a population of some four-and-a-half million persons of three classes: Spanish, Indians, and castes. Although the Spanish comprise only one tenth of the total, they possess almost all the property and wealth of the kingdom. The other two classes, nine tenths of the total population, can be subdivided into two-thirds mixed-bloods and one-third pure Indians. The Indians and castes are employed in domestic service, agriculture, the menial duties connected with commerce, and the crafts and trades. To say it differently, they are servants, menials, or day-laborers employed by the elite class. It is no wonder, then, that between them and the Spanish class there is the clash of interests and hostility that regularly prevails between those who have nothing and those who have everything, between the impoverished and the great lords. The attitude of the masses is demonstrated by envy, robbery, and indifferent labor; that of the upper class is shown by scorn, the practice of usury, and harsh measures of control. To a certain degree, these attitudes are inevitable in this situation in any part of the world. But in America the evils deriving from it are worse than they are elsewhere, for there are not gradations between classes, no middle position. There are only the rich or the miserable, the noble or the vile.

In fact, the Indians and castes are in great want and a state of degradation. Because of their color, ignorance, and misery, the Indians are relegated to a social position infinitely distant from that of the Spaniards. The laws, which theoretically eliminate this distance, prove of little advantage to them. Most of the laws, in fact, have the effect of maintaining it. Restricted to a tiny circular piece of land with a radius of 600 yards, as prescribed by the law for Indian pueblos, the Indians have no individual property. Their common lands, which they are forced to cultivate and have no immediate interest in, must be an odious burden to them. The weight of the burden, moreover, must be increasing daily because

"Estado moral y político en que se hallaba la población del virreinato de N. España en 1799, Valladolid, Dec. 11, 1799," José María Luis Mora, *Obras sueltas,* 2 vols. (Paris, 1837), I, pp. 54–68.

of the difficulty in marketing their produce, and because they are now under intendants and have no hope of getting justice except by appeal to the Superior Junta of the Royal Treasury of Mexico.

Prevented by law from marrying into the castes, the Indians are thereby deprived of the knowledge and assistance they would receive if they could trade and associate with them and with other persons. Isolated from the rest of society by their language and by a useless and tyrannical government, they perpetuate their customs, usages, and gross superstitions to such an extreme that they keep secretly eight or ten old Indians in each pueblo, who live idly at the expense of others, dominating them by the most harsh despotism imaginable. Prohibited by law from making contracts, from going in debt more than five pesos — in a word, from trading and building up credit — they cannot possibly gain in knowledge, improve their fortune, or take one step forward away from their misery. Solórzano,[1] Fraso, and other Spanish authors wondered what secret motive caused the Crown to write so many privileges into law for the Indians, and were afraid that the latter might take undue advantage of them. But it is a greater cause for wonder that these writers did not see in these same privileges great harm for the Indian. These privileges are an offensive arm that the protector of the Indians, a member of another class, can use to wound his adversary without protecting the Indians at all. The Indians are left, as a result, in a truly apathetic, inert state. They remain indifferent to the future and to almost everything that does not stimulate the base passions of the moment.

The castes that are descendants of Negro slaves are held inferior even by law. Since tribute is rigorously collected from them without exception, paying tribute has become an indelible brand of their slavery, which cannot be erased by time or the mixing of blood, no matter how many genera-

tions have passed. There are many persons among the castes who could be classed as Spaniards by their color, appearance, and good conduct. This prejudice, however, prevents their rising from the lower class. The castes are in this way discriminated against by the law. They are poor, dependent on others for their existence, and without an education that could help them. They are forced to wear the stain of their origin. Under these handicaps, they should be dejected in spirit, slaves to overpowering passions natural to their fiery nature and robust constitutions. It is no wonder that they commit many sins and crimes. It is even more a wonder that their sins and crimes are not more numerous, and that many of this caste have good customs in spite of their disadvantages.

The Indians, like the castes, are governed directly by provincial justices who have done their share to put the Indians in the circumstances I have described. Actually, the *alcaldes mayores*[2] are more like merchants than justices; they are granted exclusive rights to all trade in their territories and they use force when necessary to exercise these rights. In five years they make a profit of from 30,000 to 200,000 pesos. Their commerce with the Indians, forced on the latter at usurious prices, causes much misery for their victims. In spite of all this, there used to be two favorable circumstances. One was that the *alcaldes* disinterestedly and honestly judged in cases in which they had no personal interest. The second was that they stimulated an increase in production of manufacturing and agriculture. The government later sought to curb the worst defects of this system by prohibiting the *subdelegados,* assistants to the *alcaldes mayores,* from engaging in commerce. Since the *subdelegados* were not granted salaries, the remedy was much worse than the disease. If the *subdelegados* strictly obeyed their orders and dealt only with criminal cases, they would die of hunger because they are very poor. From

[1] Juan Pereira Solórzano (1575–c. 1653), Spanish jurisconsult, author of *Política Indiana,* famous commentary on laws of the Indies.

[2] The intendants had replaced the *alcaldes mayores* by this time.

necessity, they pervert the high purpose of their offices, defraud the poor, and traffic with criminals. For the same reason, it has been very difficult for the intendants to find qualified persons for these positions. The only applicants are those who have been failures, or those whose lack of talent or poor conduct bar them from other kinds of employment. Under these circumstances, what benefit, what protection, can these ministers of the law give to the two lower classes? How can they have a benevolent attitude toward the people they govern, or win the respect of the people, when they must resort to extortion and other kinds of injustice?

On the contrary, the priests and their assistants, whose sole purpose is to minister to the spiritual and temporal needs of these miserable classes, win their affection, gratitude, and respect. They visit and console them in their illnesses and difficulties. They must be doctors as well as priests; they prescribe medicine, buy it out of their own income, and at times even treat the patient themselves. They are the lawyers and mediators of the lower classes, taking their cases to the *alcaldes mayores* or others who take legal action against them. They defend them from the oppression of the *alcaldes mayores* and from their more powerful neighbors. In a word, the classes do not have nor can have confidence in anyone except the clergy and the superior magistrates. But appeal to the latter is very difficult.

In this state of affairs, what interest could possibly unite these two classes to the first class, and unite all three of them to the laws and the government? The first class has the utmost interest in observance of the laws that protect their lives, honor, land, and property against the assaults of the envious and the miserable. But the other two classes, without property or honor or any reason to be envied or assaulted by anyone, what have the laws to do with them? All the laws do is set forth the penalties for their crimes. What affection and gratitude could they have for the ministers of the law who use their authority only to send them to jail or the stocks or the presidio or the gallows? What ties could bind these classes to the government when they have so little evidence of its intent to protect them?

Will someone say that fear of punishment is necessary in order to keep these people in subordination to the laws and the government? A certain political writer has said that two classes make this supposition false: the rich and powerful class who break the net, and the miserable classes who slip through the meshes. If this maxim applies to conditions in Europe how much more does it apply to America where people live almost like nomads, without houses, without even an address. Modern legislators then advised that religion, which could be instilled into the hearts of these people by preaching, by advice from the pulpit, and by means of the confessional, would keep these classes in subordination to the law and the government. The priests, then, are the real custodians of the law and guarantee its observance. It is also the priests who should and do, in fact, have more influence than anyone else on the hearts of these people, and who do the most to keep them in obedience and submission to the sovereignty of Your Majesty. It is religious faith that is the most powerful tie uniting these two miserable classes, who make up nine tenths of the population, to the government.

The clergy perform services of such great importance to the government and the entire monarchy that their influence is easily more important than that of any other group. The necessity of upholding this truth and of changing the unfavorable picture that some have drawn of us, obligate me to speak out in our behalf. But the evil that threatens us is still greater. If our criticism is pointed, Your Majesty may see fit to pardon us, for if we were happier, we would speak more moderately.

We have already pointed out that the lower classes are landless, the pueblos lack property, the Indians and castes are discriminated against in practice and in theory, the judges do not protect them, and the established laws keep them isolated. At the same time, Your Majesty has been occupied with the passing of laws that are intended to bring happiness to our kingdom. Thus, it now seems only fitting and consonant with your orders for us to suggest remedies for these ills so that Your Majesty might give them his consideration. Our suggestions are made only after long meditation and the acquisition of practical knowledge about the character, temperament, usages, and customs of these people. We believe these reforms are necessary to lift them out of their misery, repress their vices, and unite them by loyalty to the government and by ties of interest to the laws. We do not intend to interfere with the sovereign judges of Your Majesty or to substitute our judgments for the wise advice of his zealous ministers. We wish only to explain certain facts that perhaps cannot be known except by persons in our position. If our suggestions might be considered and adopted, we would have the pleasure of knowing that our thoughts are in agreement with Your Majesty's. If our suggestions are not considered and adopted, we shall have had the pleasure of making a contribution to a very important matter. And in any case, Señor, we are giving testimony to our fervent desire for the most happy success in this glorious undertaking of Your Majesty.

We shall say that the general abolishing of tributes for the two classes of Indians and castes seems to us of prime importance. The second reform needed is to abolish the stigma of law that affects the castes; let them be declared honest and honorable, capable of obtaining any civil position that does not require noble blood, always providing they merit it by their good habits. The third reform needed is the distribution of all Crown-owned lands, without charge, to the Indians and the castes. The fourth reform is that the *ejidos* [common lands] of each pueblo should be divided, without charge, among the individuals of it. The fifth reform is the passing of an agrarian law like the one in Asturias and Galicia that pro-

vides for the leasing of idle lands of the great proprietors to the landless classes for periods of twenty to thirty years. The workers of the land should not be required to pay an excise tax on their produce. The law would permit enclosure of the lands, and other provisions should be passed that would guarantee this property right to the landless. Any disputes on these matters should be handled by the intendants in the first instance, with right of appeal to the Audiencia as in other civil suits. The sixth reform is to grant permission for anyone living outside an Indian pueblo — Spanish, castes, or Indians — to live in Indian pueblos and to build homes and other buildings there. The seventh reform is to grant adequate salaries to all territorial judges except the *alcaldes ordinarios,* who must serve without charge since they perform regular city council duties. If to these reforms there might be added permission to construct cotton and wool factories, this would increase the likelihood of success of the other provisions that will enable these people to take the first step toward happiness. Factories are now permitted by special license from the viceroys or governors; but this is an insuperable barrier for the poor as are any taxes and fees such as the *alcabala* and the export and import taxes.

We expect that our proposal to abolish tribute will cause surprise, given the present state of emergency of the Crown. But if in the arithmetic of the royal treasury department there are cases where three and two are not five, the present case is surely an example. And, by a reasonably accurate calculation, we shall demonstrate that by abolishing tribute and other handicaps mentioned, far from reducing income to the royal treasury, there would be an increase in less than ten years of three or four times what the tribute presently provides.

Belena,[3] in his collection of governmental decrees, asserts that the tribute from 1780–84, inclusive, was 4,439,826 pesos. This is an average of 887,975 yearly.

[3] Eusebio Ventura Belena (1736–1794).

The population of New Spain is four-and-a-half million people. Subtracting one tenth of the total, which is the Spanish class who are the most wealthy and consume the most, there remains 4,050,000 (four million and fifty thousand). At the rate of five persons per family, this would amount to 810,000 families. Some of these. families have been able by their own efforts to live decently, wearing better clothes and eating better food than the rest of their class. These would compare favorably with the lower class of Spain. About one fifth of this class are in this condition. If we suppose, however, that as many as one third of this class are in this state, 540,000 families would still be in the inferior condition. Among these, the families who are the best off are the peons on the *haciendas;* their yearly income is about fifty pesos in the regions of high altitude where the climate is cool, and about seventy pesos in the hot lands. We can then say that the average income is sixty-one pesos a year. A family in the upper one-third of this class needs at least 300 pesos for food and clothing; when this figure is compared with the sixty-one pesos, it can be seen that the income of the upper one-third exceeds by 239 pesos that of the most well off of the remaining families. On this 239 pesos the Crown would receive from the *alcabala* tax about fourteen pesos [six percent]. On this basis, if the income of the 540,000 families was increased to that of the upper one-third, the corresponding increase in the *alcabala* would be 7,560,000 pesos yearly. This means that the royal treasury would receive six times as much from this increase in the *alcabala* as it presently receives from tribute. In this way, the two thirds of the families would be relieved of their poverty, and their standard of living would be raised to that of the upper one-third. From all this it can be seen that even if the *alcabala* were considerably lowered, the income to the Crown would be three or four times that received from tribute. There would be much more income for the royal treasury, an increase in agricultural products and the volume of commerce, an improvement in customs and habits, and a resultant improvement in the quality of government.

But the royal treasury need not suffer any loss in income even while the benefits of this change are accruing. The law ordering the collection of tribute can remain in force for the first five years, or until such time as the amount of the *alcabala* has exceeded that of tribute. But actually the passing of these new laws alone would virtually bring about this increase in less time, especially if the new laws were promptly put into effect. Above all, we ask that Your Majesty accept these suggestions as the sincere testimony of our love and fidelity, and as an indication of our fervent desire to see this new legislation usher in a happy era for the greater splendor of the Spanish monarchy. Then history will place the royal author of these reforms among the Numas and Licurgos.[4]

*   *   *

We believe, Señor, we have rendered Your Majesty a very important service in setting forth the facts that appear in this discourse. We rest in complete confidence in the great virtues of Your Majesty and especially in his pious love for the church, the faith, and its ministers. We can do no more than to throw ourselves upon his clemency, to redouble our prayers to the Almighty to bring to him an understanding of our high purpose, so that by the establishment of a new code of laws he may improve his government over his vast dominions. May God protect your royal Catholic person in the greatest happiness and glory for the many years that the church and his kingdoms need him.

[4] Numenius, Greek philosopher, 2nd century; Lycurgus, Greek lawmaker, 9th century, B.C.

LIBERTY

The five readings in this second section include one from a liberal
Mexican priest of the pre-independence years of the nineteenth century,
and four from twentieth-century historians; two Venezuelans, one Chilean,
and one Spaniard. The selections show wide divergence on the question
of political liberty under the Bourbons. Even conservatives disagree on
the amount of liberty prevailing. Liberals and conservatives are in some
instances so far apart as to debate whether liberty existed, or whether
liberty was even possible because of certain Spanish character traits.
Unlike conservatives, liberals of both early and recent times argued,
somewhat inconsistently with their broad generalizations, that liberty
was at best a privilege of the classes rather than, as it ought to have
been, a possession of the masses.

The Sacred Rights of Man Have Been Crushed

MIGUEL RAMOS ARIZPE

DEFECTS OF THE SYSTEM OF GOVERNMENT

IT IS a fact as well known as it is regrettable
that the Spanish court has for three long
centuries been preoccupied with its own
aggrandizement and with that of its governors. Since it was impossible to reconcile
this aim with the liberties and economic
interests of the people, the result was a terrible conflict of interests. Power and authority conquered; the sacred rights of man
were crushed to earth. Out of this conquest
rose a system that made government synonymous with despotism, stupidity, and vice
itself. The government even prohibited the
study of natural law and society in order
that the dark night of the people's ignorance
might help support the system. Spanish
Americans, no matter how intelligent and
competent, were rarely chosen to fill government positions in or out of their own
province. Rather, the government sustained
this system by choosing Spaniards whose
chief recommendations were their subser-
vience or their influence at court or their

services to the Crown. The conquest and
subjugation of Spanish America has been
gradually carried out in these centuries of
despotism, oppression, and disgrace. And
can anyone suppose a just and liberal system would be adopted for America when in
Spain there was a desire to substitute for
the wise system of antiquity one suited for
despotism and the abasement of the liberties
and dignity of people of Spanish race? One
would have to be delirious to suppose it
would be. He who cannot govern his own
house justly cannot know how to govern
another's house well. Rather, he enters it
by force. For the sake of justice, it is sometimes necessary to face facts no matter how
much pain it may cause us. But full aware-
ness of these facts will not only convince
us that despotism has been an evil common
to Spain and Spanish America; we shall
also be convinced, as a result, that reform
of the system is necessary for the happiness
of both regions.

In America, I have only to let a Spaniard

From Miguel Ramos Arizpe, *Discursos, Memorias e Informes* (Mexico, 1942), pp. 54–77. Used by
permission of the Universidad Nacional Autónoma de México.

23

come within sight to find myself in the presence of an *adelantado* or a governor or a captain general who assumes the power of a viceroy. He is transformed into a temporary monarch who is master of all he surveys, not by the rule of law, but by the force of his will and his sword. Peace and war, the honor and property of citizens — even final rewards and punishments — all come within his purview to judge as a monarch might judge. He demands that his orders be obeyed without excuse and without asking whether the order has been signed by the king. He has been given general powers to do whatever he wishes in the name of the king and I can assure you he carries out his orders. What a system of government! Can Spain bear it even for the short time our beloved King Ferdinand may be away?

But even under this system, many of the monarchs and officials had good intentions and have attempted to moderate this monstrous power. They have ordered the establishment of city governments, *audiencias*, universities, secondary schools, and societies of learning, so that as a result enlightened citizens may be capable of defending their rights and thereby counterbalancing by their knowledge and representative institutions the power of absolutism. *Consulados*, mining guilds, and ecclesiastical *cabildos* have been established for the same purposes. The more these organizations have been influenced by the Enlightenment, the more they have become aware of their own power, and as a result have been able to temper the absolutism of a military governor.

DEFECTS OF THE GOVERNMENT OF THE
INTERIOR PROVINCES

Even after centuries, reforms such as these have left the Interior Provinces untouched. One military authority is enthroned there as occurred in Mexico during the first six years after the conquest. The provinces are ruled by a single military commander, the Commandant General, whose powers are equal to or greater than those of the Viceroy. Although the Auditor of War is supposed to exercise a check upon the Commandant General's power, he simply supports the Commandant's opinions. The official residence of the Commandant General is in Chihuahua, capital of the province of the same name, which is located about 2,000 miles westward. Trained from childhood under military discipline, and having always exercised military command, he knows nothing of civil and political laws and has an ingrained repugnance to obstacles put in his way by such laws. Here is the fundamental error of this system of government. The Commandant naturally wants to govern by the laws that he knows. He demands blind obedience almost instinctively from artisans, farmers, and stockmen. We would be rid of the evil this kind of rule causes if we were governed under civil law.

Nothing limits the power of the Commandant General. How could the Auditor of War limit it when he is the Commandant's immediate subordinate? It is a stroke of cleverness for an Auditor always to agree with his superior. And what will happen if the Commandant and Auditor become corrupt as so often does happen? They have many reasons to conspire to make money: their future needs, the impermanency of their positions, the payments they made to obtain their positions, and the costs of the long trip to their places of employment. Miserable provinces! I do not wish to name names; I know what all the provinces have experienced. I wish only to call Your Majesty's attention to how much a great and absolute authority appeals to vanity, and to how greatly the bounteous wealth of America tempts even a virtuous official.

DEFECTS OF THE LOCAL GOVERNMENT
OF THE PROVINCES

Even worse vices of government can be found in each province. The provincial governor is usually a captain, a sergeant major, or at most a colonel. And can anyone of sound mind who wants good government see how a soldier, no matter what honors he has won, can be qualified to rule on civil and economic and political matters? The only laws he knows are military ordinances; he is used to commanding a company. He knows nothing of civil law and has no lawyer to advise him. He knows nothing of the gentle character and the harmless customs of the some 50,000 farmers and stockmen over whom he has been placed. He is frequently prejudiced against them; he considers them barbarians who can be governed only by force. He should know that the climate of America is such as to tame even the ferocity of wild beasts. The greater the distance between these governors and the capital of the Commandancy General, the more despotic and irresponsible they are. Only in America could so absurd a system as the one I have described be tolerated. In fact, I am not surprised that many governors are corrupt and despotic; it is even more surprising that they have not all been tyrants under a system of government which necessarily forces them to one of two extremes: either to that of prostituting their positions, as most do, by siding with evil interests and intriguers, or losing their minds and killing themselves. Colonel Francisco Ixart of Nuevo Santander chose the latter course. His refrain while he was out of his mind was: "A man should not live who governs a province without knowing its laws." It is indeed an absurd system that places all power in a purely military command.

The truth of this statement becomes even more clear when one considers that these positions are normally obtained by bribery and chicanery. To obtain the title of governor for five years, a soldier goes into debt for fifty. He sails for America, not as a company captain or a lieutenant colonel, but with all the splendor befitting a governor; when he finally takes office, and before he has hardly had time to discover that his salary does not meet the cost of living, he receives the bills in the mail for the expenses he has incurred in obtaining the position and in making the long journey.

What can he do? The more honorable he is, the greater are his troubles. Because of his heavy debts he looks unhappy — a fact which does not escape the attention of those around him. Thus some intriguers find out how much his debts are and take advantage of the first occasion to make him a gift of money. Now the governor has lost his liberty; now justice is prostituted. The favorites make justice the blind instrument of their passions and aims. Requests for the payment of his debts again arrive and while his debts mount the governor remembers that he has a family and his tenure in office ends in five years. While meeting his debts he must maintain himself with decency, send more money to court to assure his promotion, and save thousands of pesos for his old age. Given these needs, and the fact that his salary barely permits him to exist, what would one expect the character of his government to be? How happy the provinces will be if they profit from this sad experience! It teaches that even an honest and capable official is corrupted when a system puts him in the situation I have described. One is forced to conclude that military government itself and the means of obtaining a position in it are alike absurd and prejudicial to the provinces and to the holders of office.

THE LACK OF CITY GOVERNMENT

The despotism of military government is also supported by the lack of city government. It may seem hard to believe, Your Majesty, that in the province of Coahuila, with 60,000 inhabitants, with fourteen towns of Spanish population, the only *cabildo* is in Saltillo. This statement can be verified by the document nominating me as deputy that I presented to the court. Why has no *cabildo* been established in Santa María de las Parras[1] which has 10,000 people? Why is there none in the other towns when *cabildos* are authorized by law? The answer is obvious; they are opposed by their nature to a military gov-

[1] Located 98 miles northwest of Saltillo, Coahuila state.

ernment. A military government, in keeping with despotism, needs the power of
appointment and removal of city officials
who must blindly obey it just as the city
officials must command the blind obedience
of the people. If *cabildos* were established,
which would become the fortress of the
people, and its officials were the fathers of
their own republic, the military government
would be stripped of this power.

There is also a scarcity of *cabildos* in
Nuevo León; with seventeen Spanish towns
there are *cabildos* only in Monterrey,
Linares, and Cadereyta. In the province of
Texas, the only *cabildo* is in San Antonio
de Béjar [modern San Antonio], the capital.
In spite of its twenty-nine towns and more
than 60,000 Spanish inhabitants, the province of Nuevo Santander has no *cabildo;*
worse, its towns have been deprived of even
the insignificant privilege granted them at
their founding of annually electing two
councilmen and a court representative. And
who other than the military power deprived
them of this? In 1794–95 a military com-
missioner organized militia companies in
the towns; by tacit agreement with the governor, also a military officer, in each town
the company captain was to serve as judge,
the company lieutenant and ensign as councilmen, and the first sergeant as legal representative. Vacancies would be filled by the
highest ranking militia officer available.
Thus a sergeant and even a corporal became
judges in preference to honorable private
citizens. In short, local government is a
monstrous offspring of a military system
which measures all things by the military
yardstick.

The governors are well aware that the
preemption of city offices by militiamen has
bad consequences for local government. But
they do nothing to change this, some because they fear to make any changes, others
because they are flattered by the exercise of
absolute power. Some would even destroy
the few *cabildos* in existence. I have known
of prolonged legal conflicts between the few
cabildos and the governors; I have known
more than one councilman who fled to the
mountains to avoid suffering an outrage at
the hands of a governor.

DEFECTS IN THE ADMINISTRATION OF JUSTICE

Given the few *cabildos,* the military government, and the fact that the *audiencias* of
Mexico or Guadalajara or Chihuahua are
from 800 to 2,800 miles away, a lack of justice is to be expected. Most judges are soldiers who have no one to advise them in
judicial affairs. Nor can appeals be made
from their decisions because even the near-
est *audiencia* is too far away for a person of
average means to afford the expense of an
appeal. What an aggrieved party can expect
is to be robbed of liberty, honor, and property by a local judge who hands down an
unjust decision. That he has no alternative
except to suffer such injustice is certain for
the expenses of appeal to the *audiencia*
would exceed the value of what was in dis-
pute. I have known honorable citizens to
die of the pain and grief incurred at the
impossibility of vindicating their honor or
recovering property that they were cheated
of by unjust judges. And I have witnessed
the ruin of families who chose the expen-
sive remedy of appeal. From Saltillo appeals are first made to Monclova, 240 miles
north, where the governor lives; perhaps
from there appeal is made to the Commandant General at Chihuahua, some 800 miles
to the west; or, appeals are sent 600 miles
southwest to Guadalajara to the *audiencia,*
or to the Intendant at San Luis Potosí, or
to the Superior Junta of the royal treasury
at Mexico City. And, as if there were no
storm which misses these unfortunate people, appeals on clerical matters must be sent
to the bishop in Nuevo León. From all this,
chaos and confusion result, and these honorable and deserving Spanish people live
among a thousand annoyances and grievances.

*　　*　　*

THE SUPERIOR GOVERNMENTAL JUNTA AND TRIBUNAL OF APPEALS

The nature of the government that should
be adopted must doubtless conform to the

principles of the Constitution of 1812.[2] If by those principles the dignity of man is to be proclaimed, his liberties to be recognized, his security, property and equality to be guaranteed, if he is to be governed by laws he — not despotism and tyranny — has approved, and if government and justice alike are to contribute to the well-being of the citizenry, then I ask Your Majesty, in the name of 200,000 inhabitants of the provinces, to establish there a civil government and a court of appeals. The name of the civil government will be the Superior Governmental Junta of the Four Interior Provinces of Oriente in North America; its seven members will be natives of the provinces. The basis of representation will be two members each from Coahuila, Nuevo León, and Nuevo Santander, and one only from Texas because of its small population. The judicial body will be known as the Superior Tribunal of Appeals, to be composed of an attorney and three judges, appointed by the Crown with the advice of the Council of State and the Superior Governmental Junta. Both bodies should be established in Saltillo on the understanding that they could be relocated if another site proved more suitable.

The establishment of these two bodies, moreover, conforms to the principles of a limited monarchy as provided for by the Constitution which separates the executive, legislative, and judicial powers. If these powers are separated in the supreme government in Spain, why should they not be in the provinces? Just as the king's power is limited by the Council of State and the Ministry, so should power in the four provinces be limited by the several members of both bodies rather than lodged in one person.

The Superior Governmental Junta should be composed of locally elected residents of the provinces who know the character, customs, and needs of the people, and who will give prompt attention to matters of local

importance. Prompt action by government results in general peace and prosperity. Since the Tribunal of Appeals will confine its actions to judicial matters alone, prompt administration of justice can be expected. From its central location, the Tribunal will deal impartially and wisely and promptly with the wicked; the good can then dry their tears on at last beholding a court that guarantees their liberty, property, and security. They can labor in peace for their own profit and for the general welfare of the State.

*   *   *

THE ESTABLISHMENT OF COMMITTEES IN THE TOWNS AND PROVINCES

I have made evident to Your Majesty that local government suffers most from military rule. The cure is the establishment in each province of a governmental junta or provincial deputation, and a *cabildo* in each town. By approving these institutions, Your Majesty would be showing his support of the principles supporting the rights of man. For this approval, he will receive the thanks of the people who enjoy these rights instead of being treated like slaves or sheep. These desires are general throughout the Empire; the people have demonstrated this desire since the recent removal of the yoke of slavery that has oppressed them for centuries. Hardly were the provinces orphaned by the treacherous imprisonment of King Ferdinand VII when they foresaw that Napoleon's intrigues aimed at their enslavement; they resolved to defend the liberty of the nation and ransom the king. Thus they rejected the old government and set up governmental juntas. The Central Junta of Spain, the Regency, and most recently Your Majesty have approved these actions in Spain, the Balearic Islands, and the Canaries. Government *juntas* have been established in all parts of South America except in Peru, and if it was not for the revolts in New Spain they would have been established here. Indeed, had the order permitting their establishment reached here sooner, the horrors of the civil war we are

[2] The first Spanish constitution, which reflected the aspirations of the Liberals who were in the ascendancy until 1814.

now suffering might have been avoided. But I can assure Your Majesty, as news of this has appeared in the official press of Mexico, that the loyal inhabitants of Coahuila have ejected the rebels at Monclova and, led by the able Lieutenant Colonel Simón de Herrera, have decisively defeated them in the field. Peace has been restored under a loyal *junta,* and the frontier with the United States is guarded. And from a letter I have received I know that a *junta* has been established in Nuevo León to govern that province.

The will of the people and experience recommend the establishment of this new system of government. Your Majesty can give order to this system by removing the cause for rivalries and grievances in regional relations. The need of establishing *cabildos* is so apparent that no prolonged explana-

tion is necessary. Each town is an association of free men who have come together, not to be commanded like barbarians by the strongest person, but to be governed by men wise enough to be fathers of their republic. Here is the basis for city government, formed by the laws and customs of Spain, and authorized for establishment in the Indies. Since the political virtues desired in their officials can best be appreciated by the people themselves, they should be given the right to choose them; thus despotism and selling positions at the sound of the drum [recruiting soldiers some of whom will exercise powers of government] will be abolished; the door will be opened to merit and all citizens will desire to enter. The inevitable consequence will be orderly government and the peace and happiness of the citizens.

The Gothic Shadows of the Colonial Past

ENRIQUE BERNARDO NÚÑEZ

Born in Valencia, Venezuela, Enrique Bernardo Núñez (1895–) is one of the outstanding writers of his country, a historian, man of letters, journalist, liberal, and patriot. His two-volume *City of the Red Roofs* (Caracas, 1947), a history of the capital, won the annual municipal prize for literature; in 1950, he was awarded the national prize for journalism. His other works include *Orinoco, a History of the National River* (1946), *Miranda, or the Theme of Liberty* (1950), and many essays and novels. The selection that follows is from his address in 1948 to the National Academy of History, on being received into membership.

IN RECENT times a school of historians has flourished that has attempted to find in the colonial period, not only something aesthetic like the poetry of far-off times and the origins of nationality, but a just rule, the most appropriate imaginable for the American people. Only those blinded by prejudice could fail to recognize this revisionist trend. The *Hispanistas* assure us that if their interpretation is wrong, one cannot explain how the brilliant generation of independence could have risen from a world of darkness. But the truth is that the independence generation was brilliant because it obeyed its historic destiny — to break with the past. To break with the past and at the same time remain obedient to it. It emancipated itself in the first place from the age-old discipline that the authorities wished to impose on it. To know what the colonial past really was, one would have to ask Spain itself. And its most eminent sons would reply. Both in Spain and in Venezuela a reforming generation spoke out against error, misery, and the backwardness of Spain. In both lands they felt and feel the need for a renovation of Spanish life. In both lands they felt that efforts to achieve this liberation had been frustrated. Their common enemy was the Spanish spirit that resists all the winds of change in all centuries, that opposes change with an exalted spirit in an atmosphere of Gothic shadows, prisons, and delusions. And what, if we ask ourselves, can we say the colonial past was? When it is our turn to answer, it is easy to adopt the same point of view as the Spaniards.

All one need do is keep an open mind. Thus, when one speaks of stagnation, lethargy, the decadence of Spanish civilization, we believe we are looking in a mirror gazing at our own culture. And the fact is, our national life has continued to live within this archaic mold. The symptoms of illness in Spain are signs of our own sickness. The observations of Sanz[1] could, with slight alteration, describe our condition today. Fernando de Peñalver [1765–1837], speaking at the Congress of Angostura, was astonished at what an arduous, bloody war we had to wage in order that understanding might win over the alliance of despotism and superstition. The fruits of the colonial regime are misery, ignorance, and superstition. Our people could

[1] Miguel José Sanz (1754–1814), a leader of the Venezuelan independence movement.

From Discourse of Enrique Bernardo Núñez before the National Academy of History, June 24, 1948, *La Colonia y la Independencia; juicios de historiadores venezelanos* (Caracas, 1949), pp. 151–154. Used by permission of the secretary of the National Academy of History.

be only what colonial life made them.

The fathers of independence found the reasons for rebellion in the history of America and Spain. They surveyed critically the entire colonial way of life, and whether their criticisms of it were just or not, they filed their complaints with the Spanish authorities. Even the Spanish-born residents of Venezuela made common cause with their grievances. On the other hand, the *colonialistas* see the whole colonial process as an essay on liberty. They suppose that a kind father prepared the Americans for emancipation. But the actualities of colonial life are completely contrary to this view. We find the exercise of every kind of despotism. Oviedo y Baños[2] used the restrained language of a faithful vassal in narrating the events concerning the *regidores* of Caraballeda[3] in the election of *alcaldes* of 1586, telling us that "in the colonies any act construed as opposition to the slightest whim of authority, is branded as disrespectful and classified as a crime." This was the system that prevailed in the colony. The city councils almost always ended their disputes with higher authority by yielding; it is for good reason that the Supreme Junta of Caracas informed the Regency in Spain that it had been established because "the Spanish ministry has done nothing but suppress the American *cabildos,* destroy public confidence in them, and submit them to the despotic rod of its agents." In this letter, dated May 3, 1810, there was cited part of the famous proclamation by which it was declared that the Spanish Americans must be "raised to the dignity of free men."

[2] José de Oviedo y Baños (1674–1738), a native of Bogotá, sometimes called the first historian of New Granada.
[3] Port five miles east of La Guaira, subsequently abandoned.

The loosening of imperial ties has been attributed to the diffusion of the Enlightenment, the expulsion of the Jesuits, contraband with the Antilles and foreign colonies, the capture of Trinidad by the English, and the imprisonment in La Guaira of some criminals with republican ideas. The independence of the United States and the invasion of Spain by Napoleon have also been cited as a cause for dissolution of the Empire. All this demonstrates a zeal for looking for the causes of independence outside the colonial regime. These causes, especially the last two named, could have established the right moment, the favorable climate for emancipation. But the Americans did not need to read books to learn about the burden of taxes, monopolies, and commercial restrictions. They could feel all this on their own shoulders. The burdens, not necessarily the books, are the causes for the Túpac Amaru rebellion, which was a "defensive war" as the Inca ventured to call it. The same was true of the rebellion of the *comuneros,* or communes of Socorro which the rebels tried to spread to Venezuela. And it was also true of the revolt led by Juan Francisco de León against the Basques and the rebellion in 1795 of the Negroes in Coro. Some historians try to prove that these movements had nothing to do with independence. But those who see in them the remote or immediate antecedents of independence are correct. The aspiration for liberty of commerce and freedom from oppressive taxes undermined, as no other force could, the base of the colonial regime. If one reviews the history of all peoples of the world, one will see that there is no need of books or imprisonments when the opportunity comes to throw off the yoke. Oppression is the most effective agent for liberty.

Spanish Enlightened Despotism

VICENTE PALACIO ATARD

Vicente Palacio Atard was born in Bilbao in 1920. A professor of history at the University of Madrid, he has been chiefly interested in the history of Spain during the seventeenth and eighteenth centuries. His major works include *The Third Family Pact* (1945) and *The Commerce of Castile and the Port of Santander in the Eighteenth Century* (1960).

I. THE THEORY OF ENLIGHTENED DESPOTISM

The Paradoxes of the Eighteenth Century
THE eighteenth century is full of paradoxes which are often disconcerting. Perhaps for this reason it has been difficult to comprehend the history of this century and easy to engage in passionate debates about its significance. Perhaps the greatest paradox is this: the men of the Enlightenment were obsessed with finding a solution for the main problems of society, and had a capacity for visualizing solutions that apparently exceed — as Paul Hazard says — our present capabilities. And yet the fundamental problems were treated so superficially, even frivolously, that we are surprised and sometimes indignant.

It is no cause for wonder, then, that the policy of the century — in theory and in facts — offers paradoxes. This is the sign of the times. The Enlightenment which preached liberty and the monarchs who exercised power absolutely joined hands. In contemplating this spectacle, one could become confused, supposing that because of some strange circumstance either the advocates of liberty placed themselves at the service of absolutism, or the crowned despots became champions of political liberty. Actually, the Enlightenment and Enlightened Despotism have a coincidental existence. One must not confuse them;

they are simultaneously appearing phenomena, sometimes working side by side, sometimes not doing so, but always distinct from each other. Enlightened Despotism is a manner of carrying out policy by men imbued with the philosophy of their age. This manner is sometimes in harmony with the philosophy of the Enlightenment and other times is antagonistic toward it. There were enlightened men who occupied the prime political positions of the nation and sought to impose their ideology in religious, social, economic, and political affairs. We shall see, then — although the idea cannot be applied precisely — that the two movements, the one political and the other philosophical, were rooted in the same ideological mentality. It seems as if the political fact would be a simple realization of the philosophical thought. But what happened was that ideas advanced while political systems were stationary. There may have been a moment when the enlightened ideas that carried within themselves the germ of the destruction of absolutism seized hold of the minds exercising political power. That moment would have foreshadowed the collapse of the Old Regime. But it is also true that many leaders of Enlightened Despotism had nothing to do with the philosophy of the Enlightenment. We must not draw wrong conclusions. What is included in Spanish Enlightened

From Vicente Palacio Atard, "El despotismo ilustrado español," *Arbor*, VIII, No. 22 (July-August, 1947), 27–45, 47–49, 52.

Despotism must encompass such paradoxes as the ultra-Catholic Marquis of Ensenada[1] and the Volterian Count of Aranda.

The Spanish Traditional Monarchy

During the 16th and 17th centuries, Spanish political theorists supported, almost without exception, the same doctrine: kings were vicars of God. In them were vested all temporal powers, which made them absolute monarchs. But they did not hold this power irresponsibly, nor did their holding it authorize an unlimited despotism. The doctrine stating their use of power was formulated by P. Pedro de Rivadeneyra [1527–1611] in 1595, in these words:

Earthly kings do not own their kingdoms nor are they the supreme rulers of them; rather, they are viceroys of God. And as Daniel said, "God changes epochs and eras, he removes kings and he sets up kings." Thus it behooves kings to give close attention to the instructions and orders of their King and Lord if they wish to govern in accordance with His disposition and will.

It was presumed by Quevedo or Diego de Covarrubias,[2] or any other writer of this time that royal power was subordinated to a moral norm, although it was recognized that the monarch was not subject to human laws. This was nothing but acceptance of the scholastic doctrine of the common good as the basis for civil authority, a doctrine espoused by all our political theorists including Suárez, Mariana, and especially Vitoria.[3] According to this doctrine, no political regime is a divine institution; rather, it is a human one created by the people who must themselves support it. The people, then, are sovereign and they alone by virtue of this sovereignty can legitimate civil power. This Spanish doctrinal populism, however, should not be confused with Rousseau's popular sovereignty. The liberty of man, the liberty of his conscience and will as well as his human dignity, are perfectly consecrated in the Spanish mentality. Padre Alejandro Aguado could write:

The vassals of monarchies are not slaves; their subjection is not servile. They are subject to a civil government headed by a prince who must look after the needs and well-being of those he governs.

The Bourbon monarchy that was installed in Spain in the eighteenth century recovered these theories and used them to justify its power. The intellectual foundation of the Spanish monarchy was not altered during the era of Enlightened Despotism. In Spain of the eighteenth century, there was neither a theory of the contract of government nor a theory of the social contract nor even one of the "natural order"; the legal despotism of the physiocrats was accepted. There were, indeed, fawning regalists who, apparently forgetting the traditional doctrines of the origin of power, recklessly exalted the royal function in supporting absolutism. The Spanish monarchy, in theory, was unchanged. What changed was the spirit that animated it. And this new spirit would assume form in the series of events and measures of government that together constituted the historical manifestations of Spanish Enlightened Despotism.

II. THE FACTS OF ENLIGHTENED DESPOTISM

European and Spanish Manifestations of Enlightened Absolutism

If the monarch of Enlightened Despotism was a man saturated in the philosophy of the Enlightenment, who felt paternal sympathy for the complaints and needs of all his subjects, and if this paternal sympathy motivated, as Klassen [Peter Klassen (1903–   ), German historian] suggests, his main actions, then we must declare without reservation that in Spain there was

---

[1] Cenon de Somodevilla, Marquis of Ensenada (1702–1781).

[2] Francisco Gómez de Quevedo y Villegas (1580–1645), Spanish satirist; Diego Covarrubias y Leiva (1512–1577), Spanish jurisconsult.

[3] The Spaniard, Francisco Suárez (1548–1617), theologian and philosopher; Juan de Mariana (1536–1624), historian and Jesuit; Francisco de Vitoria (1486–1546), professor of law.

no Enlightened Despotism since none of our kings of the eighteenth century learned the lessons of that philosophy. Let us now lower our gaze from the throne of the kings to the chairs of the governors. Neither do we find here a fundamental liberal policy based on the ideas of the Enlightenment. For some persons, the conclusion of Konetzke [Richard Konetzke (1897–), German Hispanist] concerning a typical man of our Enlightened Despotism will come as a surprise:

One has made an error, as so often happens in judging the enlightened princes and the statesmen of the time, if he assumes Aranda [Pedro Pablo Abarca de Bolea, Count of Aranda (1719–1798)] to be a spiritual liberator of humanity and a disciple of the thought of Voltaire and the Encyclopedists. For Aranda, the thought of the Enlightenment was the means, not the end, of power. When liberals threatened or limited the power of the monarch, he vigorously opposed them.

In the same vein, another of our leaders of Enlightened Absolutism, the Count of Floridablanca [José Moñino y Redondo, Count of Florida Blanca (1728–1808)], hastened to establish a *cordon sanitaire* when he was placed on guard by the events in France which were the outcome of these liberating ideas of the Enlightenment.

But the men of Enlightened Despotism were not always philosophers. There were, especially, certain politicians who implemented some of the measures of government. What were these measures? We shall see. Paul Hazard [(1878–1944), French historian] described the policy of the enlightened despots in this manner:

They embarked on an ample equalitarian reform program, destroying the vestiges that were still plainly visible of feudalism. Champions of progress, they carried out all provisions which they thought would bring prosperity to their subjects. The Enlightenment could be used to add splendor to their government. The administrative centralization that they carried out substituted order for the prevailing disorder. This was the order that was a reflection of universal reason; it rationalized the State.

But it is an exaggeration to say that this rationalization of the State implies a previous acceptance of rationalist philosophy. The Marquis of Ensenada was anything but a rationalist; he attempted nonetheless to carry out a rationalization of the Spanish treasury system.

There are common trends in the reform programs carried out by nearly all the European governments about the middle of the eighteenth century. In all these programs, there was a tendency for royal government to initiate reforms of the ecclesiastical organization, and to centralize the administrative organization. Common to all reform governments was a concern with the material well-being of the people; during these years, the economic doctrines of the physiocrats replaced those of mercantilism as a guide for economic development. In social reform, the tendency was to create a wider arena for the enjoyment of individual liberty by abolishing or making less burdensome all forms of servitude. There was a common desire to establish a more just tax system; among the ranks of these reformers, the single-tax advocates had many supporters. There was also in all countries a highly developed interest in cultural matters, especially in the practical application of science.

Although these broad tendencies were shared by nearly all countries, great differences between one country and another could be noted. We shall submit these general tendencies to a more minute analysis. Within them, we shall at once see a multitude of variants. For example, the village policy of Frederick II and his marked progress in legalizing sale of entailed estates cannot be compared to the protection of lands and the peasant that the men of Enlightened Despotism carried out in Spain.

Nor is the character of Enlightened Absolutism the same in all the European courts. The differences are not only in the philosophy of reform but in the character of the court itself. In the small German courts, for example, Enlightened Despotism has a markedly paternal character. Exemplaries of this variant of despotism are the courts of Charles Theodore of Dahlberg, Charles Eugene of Württemberg, Charles Augustus of Weimar, and Charles Frederick of Baden. The prince in these instances was what Pirenne [Henri Pirenne (1862–1935), Belgian historian] called the *landesvater,* the original holder of seigniorial power.

Spanish Enlightened Despotism, also, has its peculiar physiognomy, molded by a sequence of governmental measures. What runs through these, gives a tone to all of them, was the new spirit in which they were conceived and carried out. If in the previous centuries, the governments concentrated on spiritual problems and disregarded the body and its energies, in the eighteenth century, the men of our Enlightened Despotism were especially concerned with the body of Spain and its needs, without forgetting, however, the needs of the spirit. And since the body of Spain needed roads to develop its commerce, canals to irrigate its fields, industries to create wealth and raise the standard of living, these leaders built highways and roads, dug canals, developed agriculture, introduced new methods of cultivation, built factories, and encouraged the formation of large commercial companies. Did the salvation of Spain depend on this? These reforms were doubtless necessary and constituted an important goal for the men of our Enlightened Absolutism to aim at. But one should not expect such remedies to be magical. After all, the remedies of magic sometimes save the body and lose the soul.

An erudite man, who learned many things from the Enlightenment including the need to publicize and propagandize, became a spokesman for the new needs: "Spain has the gout!" exclaimed Padre Feijóo.[4] And he prescribed the remedy: "Cultivate the natural sciences as other countries do who have achieved a general

prosperity; stimulate labor, since work exalts man and produces wealth." Numerous essays were written on these subjects, and on a new teaching method, the demographic and agrarian problems, and other social questions. Campomanes, Jovellanos, and Cabarrús[5] revived the ideas of Feijóo in their diatribes against entailed estates. The reforms of Charles III are better understood when one takes into account the writings of the Benedictine.

*   *   *

Administrative Centralization

The administrative policy of Enlightened Despotism had as its aim to strengthen governmental power, to place the clergy under royal control, to increase the size of the army, and other centralizing procedures. All were attempts to increase the power of the kings, and as a result, the monarchs in Spain acquired more power than ever. The administrative institutions, which had in the past signified some authority beyond the scope of the king, either decayed or were suppressed. This was true of the Councils and the *Cortes.* The *Cortes,* except for those of Madrid, Zaragoza, and Barcelona in 1701–02, met as a single body after 1709. But this united body met only six times in the whole span of the century, and the meetings were almost solely to acknowledge the heir to the throne. The territorial councils disappeared in Aragón, Flanders, and Italy; the council of Castile, on the other hand, extended its jurisdiction over all the Spanish dominions. Other Councils, like that of the State and the Inquisition, were badly crippled. Even the Council of Castile, the highest politico-administrative organ of the country, declined noticeably; its presidents did not now serve for life, nor were they irremovable. Governors who could be removed at the pleasure of the king presided

---

[4] Benito Jerónimo Feijóo y Montenegro (1676–1764).

[5] The Spanish liberals Pedro Rodríguez, Count of Campomanes (1723–1802), Gaspar Melchor de Jovellanos (1744–1811), Francisco Cabarrús, Count of Cabarrús (1752–1810). The political theorist and economist Cabarrús was a naturalized Spaniard, having been born in Bayonne.

over the council. It could be said that by the end of the century, the government was as Desdevises du Dézert [Georges Nicolas Desdevises du Dézert (b. 1854), French historian] has described it:

Like an old, heavy ship, manned by an exhausted crew, it could keep afloat in calm water, nudged along by mild breezes, but the slightest storm would topple its masts and send it to the bottom.

The political storm was unleashed in our country in 1808; then the old vessel was wrecked. The aristocracy suffered a similar fate. Titles of nobility were multiplied and Charles III opened the ranks of the aristocracy to the bourgeoisie. Even the liberties of certain regions were suppressed, for the War of the Spanish Succession served as an excuse to abolish the municipal privileges of the kingdom of Aragón.

More and more administration was placed directly under royal power which, as a result, created a demand for more government officials. They had always been the main support for absolute monarchy. Thus new officials appeared; ministers for the central government included five and sometimes six ministers with portfolio instead of the old Secretary of Universal Dispatch. There were new ministers of State, Justice, War, Treasury, and the Indies. Intendants were appointed for territorial administration at the same time that the number of *corregidores* was increased. Royal *cedulas* of 1751 and 1760 centralized the fiscal system, eliminated the autonomy of the cities in financial matters, and placed the whole system under the supervision of the Council of Castile. The intendancies were at first only military-administrative positions but came in time to be the basis for a civil provincial administration; the municipal reforms of Charles III aimed at reducing age-old taxes charged by city governments, at bringing uniform administration to the diverse methods of city governments, and at central government control of local affairs. Dézert has noted the confusion in the provincial administration in Spain of the eighteenth century. This confusion was also a subject for ridicule by Campomanes. The division of the provinces was an anachronism for the times. Some provinces overlapped others. The picturesque case of the province of Toro was cited whose territories were widely scattered and separated from each other. The men of Enlightened Despotism wished to bring clarity, order, and reason to this confusion. They sought a more sane, manageable, and complete administrative organization. Although they could not carry out their plans completely, they laid the first stones of an edifice which was completed in the following century. It would be interesting to try to determine whether the provinces, with their new governments, were more happy than with their old, picturesque systems.

*   *   *

In all these manifestations, which point like royal banners to what we call Enlightened Despotism in Spain, we have discerned the same political tone and program of government, steadily carried out during the century, and especially during the reign of Charles III.

Charles III did not consider himself an enlightened monarch. He thought of himself, rather, as an absolute monarch; nothing would have induced him to yield any of his power. His reforms coincide — in a general way — with those of other contemporary monarchs who are considered models of Enlightened Absolutism. One could add his name to the general list. Many capable assistants lent their hands to the work he wished to do. But without initiative coming from him, without his approval, unity and continuity in the reform program would not have been possible. The king imposed these reforms in good faith because he believed they were the means of bringing happiness to his people. The old formula that defines Enlightened Despotism as "government for the people but without the people" could indeed be applied to Spain.

Liberty and the Spanish Character

ANGEL CÉSAR RIVAS

THE territory of the modern state of Venezuela was not a single political and administrative entity until the last quarter of the eighteenth century. Then there were added to the Captaincy General of Venezuela, established in 1742, the governments of Cumaná, Guayana, and Maracaibo. Still, the area was not wholly independent until 1786 when, with establishment of the Audiencia of Caracas, dependence on Santo Domingo for judicial matters was ended. Venezuela continued to be subdivided, for local government, into many small units independent from each other and governed from distant centers. This was doubtless the system of government that best suited the individualist and Levantine characteristics of the colonists — characteristics, as has been indicated earlier, that were strengthened by various influences prevailing in the colony.

When Humboldt[1] visited the Captaincy, this federative character that is so genuinely Spanish had not disappeared, notwithstanding the centralization of government carried out by the Bourbon monarchy. That indelible stamp of proud self-reliance, inherited from Spain and nourished in our environment, persisted as an individual trait that in political affairs is the spirit of autonomy. "Each family of colonists lives in almost complete isolation," the naturalist wrote. "The process of civilization cannot advance in a society of such isolated groups; but living in this way develops and strengthens the love of independence and liberty, and it has strengthened the fierce pride that distinguishes people of the Castilian race."

During the years of peace after the time of attacks by pirates, the colonists attracted a considerable number of Indians to civilization. A fusion of races took place, as in the rest of America, which was encouraged by law; not only were all mixed marriages legally sanctioned, but Castilian soldiers who married the daughters of *caciques* [Indian chiefs] acquired titles of nobility. It was not, then, unusual that the conquest of Caracas was entrusted to Fajardo,[2] a *mestizo*, nor that in later years another *mestizo*, Juan de Urquijo, was named representative of Caracas to the court in Madrid. The system of *encomiendas* contributed to the process of racial fusion; the conquistadors were given Indians so that land might have value because of their labor and so that the Spaniards might defend the land with the aid of the Indians entrusted to them. The injustice that sometimes accompanied this system was often corrected by the *audiencias* or by laws issued directly by the king.

Even before the *encomienda* system was abolished in 1687, the Spanish kings had encouraged the establishment of missions of various religious orders. The perseverance and zeal of these priests was responsible for the exploration of new regions and the establishment of Indian mission towns; so successful were these efforts that before the end of the seventeenth century, Christianized and civilized Indians, skilled in agriculture, livestock raising, and the manual arts, could colonize other parts of Venezuela.

By the beginning of the seventeenth

[1] Friedrich Heinrich Alexander, Baron von Humboldt, 1769–1859, German naturalist and traveler.

[2] Francisco Fajardo (?–1564).

From Angel César Rivas, *Ensayos de Historia y Política y Diplomática* (Madrid, 1916), pp. 61–67, 77–78, 82–87, 119, 154–160.

century, after long and arduous labors by conquerors and colonists, Venezuela had emerged from the era of Osorio.[3] Encouraged by Philip II, the *cabildo* of Caracas had established in 1593 a primary school in that city; primary schools were also founded in other towns of the colony. In addition to these schools, convents and churches established various other schools, and some colonists' sons were educated in Santo Domingo. The establishment in 1673 of the Seminary of Caracas is proof that government income was then much more than it had been in 1592 as was, without doubt, the level of knowledge of the inhabitants. Aldecir de Oviedo, who came to Caracas during these years with his uncle, bishop Baños,[4] spoke of the Venezuelans as "speaking Castilian perfectly, not the poor grammar that is heard in the ports of the Indies; all are so inclined toward receiving an education that even the Negroes (born in Venezuela) hold one in disdain who does not know how to read or write." An ecclesiastical *cabildo* was in existence in Venezuela from the earliest times and all the rectors of churches throughout the area were doctors in canon law or theology. This we know from a list of priests who in 1687 drew up the famous synodal constitutions of the diocese of Caracas.

We find that during these years various social groups and classes had been formed. Each was zealous in protecting whatever rights and privileges it possessed. Doubtless the most interesting aspect of public life then was the disputes and rivalries over matters of protocol at public affairs that exercised public officials and private persons. A small group of descendants of the conquistadors occupied the first rank in Venezuelan colonial society; among this group were a number of *caballeros* descended from noble families of Castile. Others had risen to this rank as a result of the contribution of their forefathers in the conquest. Over the centuries, this group was enlarged by the marriage of its daughters with various of the governors and other royal officials who came from Spain.

The heads of the main families of this group held without interruption during the seventeenth century the offices of municipal government; those who had privileges of nobility also retained them throughout this time. Since they had exercised this leadership, passing it on from generation to generation, they were accustomed to carrying out the highest responsibilities of local government. Later, when their financial condition permitted the more serene and sober life of great lords and the acquisition of titles, some of them, proud of their heritage and conscious of their importance to their community, purchased titles of marquises and counts from the king. In May, 1698, for example, Charles II granted to D. Juan Mixares de Solórzano the Castilian titles of marquis and viscount of Mixares. The king was prompt to satisfy the vanity of others by promptly rewarding outstanding service, thereby officially confirming the gratitude the local people had already shown toward those who had sacrificed themselves on the altar of public causes. The king's actions gave royal sanction to the affection and appreciation which the local inhabitants felt toward those who had formerly defended them, carried out matters in the public interest, and protected their rights and privileges.

These men, in fact, administered justice as *alcaldes*, dealt with our municipal affairs as *regidores*, formulated local laws, determined how city income would be spent, planned and carried out public works, and established and kept in force municipal liberties. In times of insecurity, they took up arms, commanded the local militias, and met the expenses of defense out of their own incomes. In reality, it was to the king's interest to exalt this leading class of one of his dominions; in his eyes, they were at once the best guarantee of law and order and of his prerogatives of sovereignty.

[3] Diego Osorio, governor of Venezuela from 1587 to 1597, during a period of factional strife.

[4] Diego Baños y Sotomayor (?–1706), a native of Bogotá.

Thus, when the eighteenth century began, all the requisites for a nation had already been met in Venezuela. Lapouge[5] sums these up in this way:

The birth of a historic people demands the presence of a superior ethnic element, capable of directing and controlling the masses. These elements, whether in antiquity, the Middle Ages, or our own times, whether in our own or a foreign civilization, are normally the descendants of a conquering people.

Now, if more proof is wanted of the autonomy that the Venezuelan municipalities enjoyed, and of the zeal with which the sons of the conquistadors guarded the privileges of those civic bodies, this proof is given us in the events that disturbed the government in 1725. In that year, the ordinary *alcaldes* of Caracas, who had requested and obtained from the Audiencia of Santa Fe the necessary order, deposed and imprisoned Governor Portales. Their exercise of power did not even stop with this; when the bishop, Escalona, managed to have the governor freed from prison, an act authorized by a royal *cedula* of May 5, 1724, the city officials refused to permit Portales to resume command. When Portales tried to secure the obedience of the inhabitants outside the capital, the councilors organized an army of 800 men and marched toward Valencia to capture the governor. To restore order in the province, it was necessary for the king to issue *cedulas* on July 18, 1725, and January 21, 1726, ordering the reinstatement of Portales, fining the *regidores* and *alcaldes* 1,000 pesos, and ordering that they be sent to Spain for trial.

[By 1777], the energy of Venezuela's sons, invigorated by the spirit of enterprise contributed by the Basques, had succeeded in creating the conditions of material prosperity, of social health, and general vigorousness which were a result of the prevailing liberty; within the next twenty years

alone, the Venezuelans would show themselves to be a people of exuberant virility, avid for glory, conscious of their destiny, and motivated by the most expansive sentiments. On her part, Spain perfected this great secular work by giving the colony a harmonious administration that was adequate for the growing importance of the colony.

The organization of the Captaincy in 1777 gave it the administrative character of the large Spanish colonies in America. Within this administrative organization, the Spanish monarchs, who were not suspicious of local political power, permitted the creation of deliberative bodies before which the Venezuelans discussed their interests and needs or brought their pleas and complaints. This was permitted regardless of the fact that such bodies foreshadowed the decline of absolutism. In 1786, the Audiencia of Caracas was established which permitted the Venezuelans to seek justice without the need of great expense and trouble; the *audiencia* proved a bulwark for municipal rights against the encroachment of the authorities, and a training school where the lawyers and jurisconsults of Venezuela could apply their knowledge and prepare for duties connected with the new political system of the future. They were, in fact, becoming familiar with a judicial code which would survive in Venezuela for some fifty years after independence. A little later, in 1791, the king authorized the founding of the College of Lawyers in Caracas; the constitution of the college was the work of local lawyers themselves. From this college the many statesmen would be graduated who would give form and direction to the new nation of the future, and who would be famous in the life of the early Republic.

*   *   *

What was still lacking in the picture of colonial administration was, it is true, a liberty which would harmonize with that *ambiente* of autonomy that new people

[5] Georges Vacher de Lapouge (1854–1936), French sociologist.

acquire as a result of their own labors; this liberty would be no more than the formal recognition of a quality acquired in the course of a long and painful incubation. But this kind of liberty, indispensable for the life and dignity of nations — especially for their life — did not exist even in Spain. As we have said before, a vigorous liberty was upheld in the kingdoms of Castile and Aragón; the conquistadors brought it to America where it was infused in the municipal ordinances; their sons defended it resolutely during many years even when in Spain the monarchs had overturned the altars to this goddess. As we have shown, the Venezuelan *cabildos* conserved the old and sacrosanct cult of liberty for more than a century so that when the rude hand of the central power suppressed the resistance of the city councilmen, the grief felt because of that insult united with radiant hope for a future vindication in the soul of the colonists.

In fact, on every opportune occasion, the *cabildos* tried to recover the ascendancy that they had enjoyed. When the inhabitants of towns adjacent to Caracas rebelled against the Guipúzcoa Company, the Caracas municipality appointed several *regidores* to confer with the leaders of the rebellion; they joined with those leaders to hear, in the manner of a tribunal, their complaints and helped to draw up the complaints that ultimately would destroy the monopoly itself. Later, in 1769, the councilors of Caracas discussed with the Captain General the right to organize militia without his consent, doing so, as he informed the king, "without that respect and veneration demanded by custom and law." Governor Solano then named D. Sebastián de Miranda, captain of a battalion of militia. The councilmen later complained to the monarch that the governor was careless in carrying out matters important for the common good.

Again, the *ayuntamiento* gave signs of its old vigor in 1779 when it requested abolition of the tobacco monopoly, and in 1793, when it called an open *cabildo* to discuss measures connected with the proposed abolition of that monopoly.

At the time the colony achieved that level of development I have described, which was due to the privilege of free commerce, there occurred in Europe the event which was to have repercussions around the world. Its effect in Venezuela was to revive the spirit of liberty in the *cabildos,* to kindle the desire for liberty and independence in the hearts of the majority of the inhabitants — a desire that was in harmony with their inherited beliefs, was supported by their isolated condition and by their physical environment. We refer to the great movement that the heroes of liberty had begun in favor of popular rights and to the tremendous revolution which broke out after 1793. It was formed of several currents of thought and made up the content of the preaching and teaching of countless men of the age. One aspect was the mere planting of the seed of liberty as occurred a century earlier in England; but the movement looked toward the annihilation of the absolute power of kings, the integrity of individual guarantees, and the consecration of the most capable men regardless of the conditions of their birth or their social status. Another current of thought pointed to deeper and wider consequences; it rested on the premise of the natural equality of man and on the fiction of a contract that no one has yet discovered, and it proposed to destroy everything that symbolized hierarchy in a society, everything that stood for tradition, and to enthrone a government resting on sentiment and reason — the perfect and absolute leveling of humanity.

The first of these tendencies was not new to people of Spanish origin; their past was an abundant source of this kind of liberty. Nor were the doctrines concerning the limitation of royal power and the direct participation of the people in public matters cause for astonishment. The memory of the old Spanish *Cortes* was not forgotten. Just as the spirit of municipal liberty survived in Spain as evidenced in Catalonia during the reign of Philip IV, so did the municipalities of America struggle to reconquer a state of political vigor that was only recently and slightly diminished. They could not have forgotten those maxims of government that Spanish theologians and jurists had expounded precisely and justly on many occasions in the past. Long before the French Encyclopedists flourished, Soto and Suárez[6] had proclaimed that sovereignty lies not in any particular man but in men as a political body, and that the people delegate their power to the prince who can be relieved of it if he become a tyrant. Without risking the dangers he would have to suffer in France, Mariana[7] could publish in Spain about 1599 his famous treatise, *De Rege et Regis Institutione,* in which he fearlessly defended the doctrine of tyrannicide. In this work one meets such ideas as:

The king exercises moderately the power he receives from the people . . . thus, he does not dominate his subjects like slaves as tyrants do; rather, he governs them as free men should be governed. Having received power from the people, the king strives to maintain the good will of his people during his entire lifetime.

Whoever thinks the political philosophies that began to transform the English and French people from the seventeenth century lacked roots in Spain is seriously mistaken. On the other hand, it is easy to show that the Encylopedists had disciples and enthusiastic imitators in Spain since the early part of the century. It is easy to show that more than one of the ministers of Charles III introduced ideas contained in French thought into the government, and that from the beginning of the eighteenth century, the men who won the greatest renown and exercised the greatest influence on public opinion, were those who, in their books and other writings, attacked the scholastic tradition. These books, whose circulation in Spain the authorities did not interfere with, passed as easily to the Indies,

Mexico, Peru, New Granada, and Venezuela. When Humboldt visited us in 1799, he saw the works of many of these Spanish writers; the books were not only in urban homes but in those in the mountains of Caripe[8] and on *haciendas.* They were always regarded by their owners as a refuge from despotism. "I stayed," he wrote, "in the cell of a Guardian where there was a large collection of books that included the *Teatro Crítico* of Feijóo, the *Cartas Edificantes,* and the *Tratado de Electricidad* of Abbot Nollet."[9] The works of the Encyclopedists were read in the capitals of the province and in small towns years before the Estates General gathered in France. In 1786, the Count of Ségur visited the colony; on his way to Caracas he stopped in La Victoria, where he met a doctor who took him to his house and showed him, with great pleasure, the works of Rousseau and Raynal.

*   *   *

The abnormal situation prevailing in Spain after 1797 was certain to cause unrest in the Captaincy General. The absence of regular communication with Spain was to awaken in all classes, but especially in that of the patricians, the desire — always near the surface — to reconquer their liberties. The descendants of the *regidores* and *alcaldes* of the sixteenth and seventeenth centuries were soon to conquer the preponderant position that their forefathers had enjoyed, and the old winds of liberty, freed as the barriers to the initiative of the *cabildos* came down after some sixty years, set in motion by the uprising felt around the world, lashed with the sudden fury of a southwest wind against the secular fortress, where, from the ramparts, the flag of Castile floated — serene and majestic.

*   *   *

It has been endlessly repeated that Spain enslaved and degraded the descendants of the discoverers. But the events of history

---

[6] Domingo de Soto (1494–1570) and Francisco Suárez (1548–1617).

[7] Juan de Mariana (1536–1624), historian and Jesuit.

[8] Sucre State, northeastern Venezuela.

[9] Jeon Antoine Nollet (1700–1770), French physicist.

are contrary to this view. The testimony of famous foreign travelers all are in agreement with the statement made, on the eve of independence by the captain of the warship *Beaver* to his government:

These inhabitants are not in any manner that indolent and degenerate race we find in the same latitude in the Orient; far from it, they seem to have all that intellectual vigor and energy of character we have considered distinctive of the inhabitants of the more northern regions.

Perhaps the accusation against Spain is explained by an inadequate study of the period; perhaps the accusers have accepted as the conclusions of history the opinions born in the heat of the great war [for independence], those commonplaces of patriotic literature; or, perhaps this criticism contrasts the degree of liberty written in documents and actually effective in the colony, with the idea of liberty inspired by revolutionary propaganda that the critics give an exaggerated importance to, considering independence as the results of its influence alone. Neither fact nor scientific knowledge justifies this judgment.

The eclipse of liberty was common to Spain and America. What we understand by the word "liberty" today was the same condition enjoyed centuries ago by the Castilians and Aragonese. For both ourselves now and our ancestors then personal government and the abuses that spring from it were a source of serious problems. It is hardly logical, then, to state that one was denied advantages which the other possessed. And, a curious thing, while administrative disorders were equally harmful to both, Venezuela enjoyed, as did the other colonies, the government of honest and enlightened magistrates who placed her on the path of progress. The names of Pimentel, Osorio, Berroterán, Sucre, Diguja, Centurión, Solano, Saavedra, Casa-León, Guillermi, Emparán,[10] and many others

will suffice to support our statement.

The undertaking of emancipation evidently was a bold revelation of character rather than an action inspired by a mere idea; Lapouge tells us: "The historic superiority of a race consists more in character than in intelligence." The same sociologist adds that "although the superiority of an energetic race cannot endure without the aid of intelligence, the latter alone guarantees nothing but intelligent subordinates who are helpless when their commander is absent." "The character of a people, not their intelligence," says Le Bon,[11] "determines their evolution in history and regulates their destiny."

The creoles who from the beginning exercised command, who established municipal government, who defended it against absolutism and centralism, were the same colonists that resurrected from oblivion the old supremacy of the *cabildos* and proclaimed independence. They were essentially Spanish, by race, by tradition, by custom. They were the descendants of the daring and energetic conquistadors who braved unknown seas to conquer a continent; they were the descendants of those who had acquired the precious gem of liberty, of those who in eight centuries had reconquered the fatherland by courage and tenacity, and who laid the basis for the greatest empire in the world.

Just as the intellect is the exclusive product of an education necessarily restricted by a lifetime, character, which normally resists and escapes the influence of education, is not itself established except when the materials that comprise it come into being, as they do in the synthesis of the perduring feelings of a race, transmitted by heredity — like the monogram of a moral patrimony — across the centuries. The colonists received a new conception of the state from the French *philosophes* and Encyclopedists; in the political turmoil that transformed European society in accordance

[10] Governors of Venezuela. Besides Osorio, mentioned earlier, available data permit identification of the following, with their terms of office: Juan

de Pimentel, 1576–83; Francisco de Berroterán, 1693–99, 1705–06; Vicente Emparán, 1809–10.
[11] André Le Bon (1859–1938), French historian.

with a grandiose ideal perhaps they found
the incentive for realizing a great work.
But what no foreigners could transmit was
surely the perseverance, that saw them rise
again after defeat with renewed and more
powerful vigor, the strength of will that
placed them above grief and misery, the
zeal for sacrifice that induced them to seek
a heroic death in winning for posterity an
independent country, and the tenacity that
conquered all obstacles in fourteen years
of Homeric struggles.

It has often been observed that in the
process of formation and development of
races, the mentality undergoes mutations
and changes; this suggests the conclusion
that there are no immutable feelings differ-
entiating one race from another. And as
Le Bon indicates,

that is how the sociological species is formed in
the same manner as other forms of life by an
extremely minute number of irreducible basic
characteristics with accessory characteristics,
susceptible to change, grouped around them.

The circumstances of environment and
time could on occasion produce colonists
of Spanish origin who were apparently
docile servants at the caprice of their sovereign, men devoid of initiative or a sense
of civic values. But it should be observed
that after this temporary period, common to
all peoples, those basic character traits
cause an irruption, dikes are broken, a tor-
rential river overflows, and the people sometimes succeed in changing the very face of
things, in altering the previous course of
events. Then it seems that we are witness-
ing an event, cut off from the past, which
gives birth to new men, unknown entities,
creatures of an unknown culture. Behind
the recently acquired forms that we have
momentarily fixed our gaze on, however,
there reappears the essential character of
the race. And, compared with this appearance, the belief in sudden transformations,
the seeking of flattering explanations in the
insecure domain of Chance or Destiny, are
only passing dreams or vain efforts.

The emancipation of the colony was for
some time contemporary with the Spanish
rebellion against Napoleon, and in the
vicissitudes of these two movements, it is
easy to find identical characteristics: the
same intrepidity, the same indomitable tenacity, the same love bordering on delirium
for a free country. If these were the gifts of
the mother, in whose veins flowed a noble
blood, they would be surely exhibited in the
daughter without scorn.

Spain had created in Venezuela the
material wealth indispensable for the great
efforts of the liberators; it was that wealth
which nourished the legion of outstanding
men, captains, statesmen, diplomats, ministers of the treasury, magistrates, and
writers who from the beginning and
throughout the war established and fi-
nanced the new State.

From the mother country, they inherited
the strength that never for a moment failed
them in the realization of their plans; from
her they also received the fabric of society
since the civil legislation in force in the
colony continued to be the guardian of
individual rights, the tutelary goddess of
the family and the hearth.

The great figures of the epic poem of
emancipation should not be termed either
ingrates or oppressors. They had to rely on
force to become independent; certain of
them furnished by their blood, their education, and their substance the elements of
that force. If in the past, hatred caused
insults and recriminations, the historian
cannot indulge in such sentiments nor
should they be in our hearts at the present
time. As Renan[12] affirms:

the most dangerous error is to believe that one
serves his country by slandering those who
founded it. All the centuries of a nation's life
are leaves in the same book. The real leaders
of progress are those men who take as their
point of departure a profound respect for the
past: all that we do, all that we are, is the
result of the labor of those who have lived
before us.

[12] Ernest Renan (1823–1892), French philosopher.

If the capitulation signed in Ayacucho could have ended the hecatomb, could have resulted in a cordial and honorable embrace of two great branches of the same human family, a Spaniard might have been able to disperse the smoke of the battlefield, perhaps might have been able to greet the event with a show of pride. Perhaps the mother and the daughter might have celebrated their grandeur together, might have spoken the eulogy that years later, on contemplating the strength of England and her transatlantic daughter, Gladstone uttered as he recalled Horace:

Oh strong mother of a daughter stronger still!

The Political Ascendancy of the Creoles

JAIME EYZAGUIRRE

Jaime Eyzaguirre (1908–   ), one of the outstanding historians of his country, was born in Santiago de Chile. An active historian for more than three decades, he is professor of legal and constitutional history at the University of Chile and the Catholic University of Santiago. He is a member of the Chilean Academies of Language and History and is Secretary and Director of the *Boletín*, official publication of the latter institution. His many published works include a biography of the independence leader, *O'Higgins* (1946), which won first prize in the National O'Higgins Conference of that year; *Historical Physiognomy of Chile* (1948); *Chile During the Government of Errázariz Echaurren, 1896–1901* (1957); and *Ideario y Ruta de la Emancipación Chilena* (1957), from which the following selection is taken.

NEW POLITICAL ORIENTATIONS

IN EUROPE in the seventeenth century, the continual wars which Spain rarely won, the permanent separation of Portugal and the attempted separation of Catalonia, the economic prostration, the ineptness of the last Habsburg, Charles II, whose empire was dismembered after his death as a result of the War of the Spanish Succession — all these matters caused a profound pessimism in the Spanish soul. Spaniards were convinced that the nation was decadent. Despair prompted reappraisals by various writers who sought to diagnose the ills that inflicted the country and to offer remedies for them. Reason and progress challenged an inert tradition. France was the chief model.

More pragmatic than philosophic, this new outlook was responsible for putting the financial system in order, stimulating education, developing industry, increasing the volume of commerce, and carrying out public works. The Crown was considered the executive arm of all these undertakings; for this reason, the government was given greater power in order to carry them out, a tendency easily reconciled with the bent of the new Bourbon dynasty, which inaugurated the eighteenth century in Spain.

In fact, the old national political doctrine that conceived of the State as the harmonious uniting of two disparate entities — Crown and people — was gradually yielding its place to the French theory of the divine right of kings. Now the monarch received his power directly from God without the mediation of any community of people. Now the king accounted only to God for his acts, which were to be performed for the benefit of the people, who passively received the king's favors.

The formula of Louis XIV, "I am the state," constituted for the descendants of Philip V, the Bourbons of Spain, not so much a doctrine that they believed in as a norm of government they found necessary to practice. Centralization of power was gradually implemented in the political life of the nation. The Crown of Aragón lost its distinctive political personality and was

From Jaime Eyzaguirre, *Ideario y Ruta de la Emancipación Chilena* (Santiago, 1957), pp. 44–45, 52–58. Used by permission of Editorial Universitaria, S.A.

annexed as a province of Castile. The intendants were established in Spain and the Indies as direct agents of the king. The powers of the Councils were weakened and gave way in importance to secretaries whose titles were issued directly by the monarch. The Council of the Indies was bypassed in most of the matters it formerly handled; these were taken over by the Secretaries of the Navy and the Indies, who were members of a Secretariat which underwent various changes till 1790. After that year, American affairs were not handled by special ministers but were assigned to various of the Secretaries of State depending on the nature of the matter. In this way the Hispano-American monarchy, based on a plurality of kingdoms, was altered by a slow process of centralization, making it only natural to refer to the former kingdoms as "dominions." The old conception of the patrimonial monarchy, diverse kingdoms tied together by common loyalty to the king, had given way to the idea of a national monarchy.

*   *   *

From the Patrimonial State to the National State

The noticeable displeasure shown in various parts of America at the expulsion of the Jesuits was one indication of the changing personality of the king's subjects overseas; the significance of this change did not escape some of the astute ministers in Madrid. Prompted by information received from Mexico, the Madrid government held an extraordinary council on March 4, 1768. The Count of Aranda presided and those attending included the state attorneys Campomanes and Moñino, the future Count of Floridablanca.[1] The purpose of the meeting was to discuss the serious problem of how to improve relations between

[1] Pedro Pablo Abarca de Bolea, Count of Aranda (1719–98); Pedro Rodríguez, Count of Campomanes (1723–1802); José Moñino y Redondo, Count of Florida Blanca (1728–1808).

the government and the Indies. In the opinion of the last two statesmen mentioned, something should be done to counteract the idea prevailing in America that the Madrid government was concerned only with getting as much as it could out of the overseas holdings, and Spaniards who came to the New World were motivated only by a desire to get rich at the expense of the Americans. To disarm this prejudice and cause the Americans to love the mother country, the ministers believed it was necessary to tie them to Spain with strong ties of interest. The two attorneys stated:

It is today urgent to attract the Americans to Spain by means of a study program and by an honorable and intellectually brilliant institution for this purpose, and to give them a certain number of positions in the army. We should have a regiment of American-born soldiers in the peninsula, and should retain the policy of sending only Spaniards to America to fill the main ecclesiastical and political positions and of filling the equivalent positions in Spain with creoles. This is what will strengthen our ties of friendship and union, and will make of the nation one body, for the creoles here will be like so many hostages who will help keep those countries under the just rule of Your Majesty.

In accordance with this reform program, a Royal Order of February 21, 1776, instructed the Ministry of Castile to propose American candidates for positions in the church and the legal system of Spain and instructed the Ministry of the Indies to nominate Spaniards for corresponding positions in the New World with the qualification that "there will always be reserved one-third of the canonries and prebends of the cathedrals there for the Spanish Americans." In the same year, the viceroys and governors of America were notified that creoles could enlist as cadets in the regular army corps stationed in America, and would be subject to the same promotional system as native Spaniards. By a royal order of April 6, 1793, a company of American *caballeros* was established as part of the Corps of Royal Guards; in 1792, an order authorized founding of the Royal College in Granada for American nobles.

In the extraordinary council of 1768, and in the measures subsequently passed, there can be observed a tendency to eliminate the old conception of the monarchy under which the Indies and other kingdoms of Spain were parts of the royal patrimony held together by their ties to the king. The rising prosperity of the overseas provinces caused the Madrid government to fear, with reason, that the pronounced localist spirit in evidence there would generate a serious conspiracy against the unity of the great monarchy. The Spanish statesmen would offset this danger by creating ties between America and Spain which would cause a gradual transformation of the patrimonial state into a national one.

Although the plans were carried out, it was impossible to achieve the desired results. The creole's strong love for his native land, the awakening at this time of a national feeling, accentuated his fondness for the *patria chica* and made him oblivious to the broad national vision of the Spanish monarchy. The old quarrel between creoles and Spaniards over the apportionment of the official positions in the Indies, which had begun under the Habsburgs, continued and was intensified under the Bourbons in spite of the fact that the creoles obtained an undoubted predominance in the bureaucracy in America and obtained worthy honors in Spain. Whoever reads declarations like that of Francisco José Marán, the bishop of Concepción, could conclude that creoles rarely acquired high positions in the church. In 1786, Bishop Marán wrote to the bishop of Santiago, Manuel de Alday, that he was afraid he would be refused a transfer to the sea of Arequipa, his native city, because of "the original sin of being born in the Indies." Aside from the fact that the complaining bishop was actually granted the bishopric in Arequipa, just as he had been earlier granted one in Concepción without his

American birth disqualifying him in either case, it is worth noting that of nine bishops at Santiago de Chile between 1708 and 1807, and eight bishops of Concepción between 1706 and 1806, only two at each place were Spaniards. It is true that the majority of creoles who held these positions were not born in Chile, but at the same time nine native Chileans were granted bishoprics in other parts of the New World between 1701 and 1810.

What has been said of the church is also true of positions in the civil government and the army. Barros Arana[2] made a note on this point in his great *Historia:*

We found several *legajos* in the Archive of Simancas containing service records of officers, who in the last years of the 18th century and first years of the 19th, served in Chile in the regular army and the militia. We examined the documents in detail and made copies of many of them. The militia officers were, with few exceptions, native Chileans; in the regular army about half the officers were Chilean creoles. These data do not permit us to accept as unquestionable truth the charge often made that Spain systematically prohibited creoles from following a military career.

The positions in the *audiencias* during the second half of the eighteenth century were in the majority filled by Americans. In 1816 an apologist for Spanish rule could easily draw up a list of thirty-six native *oidores* of South America who held positions in the *audiencias* of America and Spain. Thirteen of these lawyers were native Chileans and three of them held high positions in Spain.

In Chile, as in many other regions of the continent, the creoles had an undoubted position of hegemony in the bureaucracy on the eve of independence. It is enough to recall that in September, 1810, when a *junta* was established in Chile, native Chileans held the following positions in the country: Don Mateo de Toro Zambrano,

[2] Diego Barros Arana (1830–1907), Chilean historian.

interim governor of the kingdom, Don José Antonio Martínez de Aldunate, bishop-elect of Santiago; Don José de Santiago Concha and Don José Santiago Martínez de Aldunate, *oidores* of the Royal Audiencia; Don José Santiago Portales, Superintendent of the Mint; and Don José Gaspar Marín, assessor of the Captaincy General.

In view of these facts, it is impossible to accept the argument so often resorted to that the revolution for independence was provoked by the unjust exclusion of creoles from public office. The truth is that the bureaucratic hegemony of the creoles was, at least after the middle of the eighteenth century, well established. But the patrimonial concept of the State, an idea creoles held dear, caused them to aspire not to the majority of the positions in their kingdom but to a monopoly of them. They felt that Spaniards should be entirely excluded. The creoles revealed this feeling in a presentation to the king in the city of Mexico on May 2, 1771. Far from complaining of the exclusion of the creoles from the primary civil, ecclesiastical, and military positions, the councilmen frankly stated:

we should not weary your Majesty by informing him of the various claims being made that natives should not only be preferred for all honorable public positions in the country but should hold these positions exclusively, without sharing them with foreigners.

The utilitarian basis as a support for the national monarchy was much favored by Campomanes. But it was inadequate to create ties between America and Spain. The affectionate disposition of the colonists, which is part of their Spanish nature, was not satisfied with the practical gains that might have satisfied people of Saxon origin. In the Habsburg period, the expansion of the Christian faith and its defense against heresy was the kind of powerful idea linked with feeling that could unite the separate wills of the kingdoms of Spain and the distant kingdoms overseas, could attract national adherence to a policy, and give solidarity to a monarchy scattered around the world. In the century of Reason, a policy linked with divine purposes had no place, and the pragmatism that was substituted for it left hearts untouched and wills inert. Only one source of inspiration was still effective and was capable of uniting Spaniards and Americans into a single force: reverence for the king. But Bourbon absolutism had carried exaltation of the monarchy into the realm of divinity. A group of kingdoms which were becoming more and more aware of their difference from Spain were still held in the monarchy by the myth of the divine right of kings. What could hold them in the monarchy if even this idea were discredited?

FAITH

The four readings in this last section include two from nineteenth-century Colombian writers, one liberal, the other conservative, and two from historians of the present century, one a Mexican conservative and the other a Spanish moderate. About the fundamental issue—the conflict between liberty of thought and religious faith—these writers show great differences in choice of detail and approach, and in their relation of the Bourbon reformers to that conflict. All of them have lived through bloody civil wars that have necessarily charged this issue with great emotion.

Jesus Christ and Jeremy Bentham

DR. VICENTE AZUERO

Dr. Vicente Azuero, about whom little is known, was a professor of law in Bogotá during the years immediately following independence. A well-educated liberal, he served as an adviser on education to Vice-President Francisco de Paula Santander, and in 1825 served on the three-member National Committee on Education appointed by the Vice-President to produce a uniform curriculum for the school system. His enthusiastic support for the teaching of Jeremy Bentham's *An Introduction to the Principles of Morals and Legislation* and his membership in the Colombian Bible Society caused him to be attacked from the pulpit by the priest, Dr. Francisco Margalló, who had formerly been his teacher in theology. Azuero's letter to the Vice-President constitutes a stout defense of Bentham's doctrines, a condemnation of Dr. Margalló, and an eloquent statement of the liberal point of view on freedom of thought and conscience.

MOST EXCELLENT SIR: Although it is very unpleasant for me to do so, I must tell Your Excellency about an event that may seem unimportant, but one can easily imagine the bad effects of it on the future of the country. Perhaps I shall succeed in making this important truth clear so that it will merit the careful attention of the supreme government. Then surely the government will take whatever measures are necessary for the good of the country; to operate be-fore the disease has gone very far is much better than to wait, for remedies applied tardily are always ineffective and painful.

During the last few weeks of Lent, I have been the object of an infamous attack by a factious cleric who disobeys the laws of the Republic. I should say that I personally have not been attacked as much as the wise system of education that the government established for Colombian youth. During Lent, Doctor Francisco Margalló,

Letter of Doctor Vicente Azuero to V.P. Francisco de Paula Santander, Bogotá, April 11, 1826, José Manuel Groot, *Historia eclesiástica y civil de Nueva Granada*, 5 vols. (2nd ed., rev.; Bogotá, 1889–1893), V, vii–xxiv.

sacristan of Las Nieves, a parochial church in this city, attacked the principles of civil and criminal law advocated by the famous English jurist, Jeremy Bentham [1748–1832]. In the Church of the Third Order [lay congregation led by Dominicans], where he conducted services for some forty persons, he said angrily:

The *colegio* of San Bartolomé is a nursery of impiety and heresy that shall be burned down. How I wish it would happen tonight!

He especially denounced the Chair of Public Law and the teachings of Bentham; he informed his audience that Benthamite doctrines were impious and those who adopted them were thereby excommunicated. I received special mention as one who had been his pupil in theology but had become perverted by the influence of bad company and bad books. He described the *colegio* as a school of corruption. In the monastery of Santa Gertrudis he made similar comments before a large audience. On the night of March 18th, which was Saturday of Holy Week, he suddenly appeared among a group of students of the *Colegio* of San Bartolomé and delivered a violent harangue against the study of Bentham, saying that his works were prohibited by the bull *In coena Domini*, and that those teaching and following his principles are excommunicated. He intends to make his parishioners hate the teachings of Bentham on the grounds that they are incompatible with Christianity; he puts the question to them as if it were a choice: Jesus Christ or Jeremy Bentham? He again mentioned me on this occasion, saying that I had fallen into error of my own free will.

In order that the full implication of the criminality of these acts be understood, I should not omit that Your Excellency signed a law on July 28, 1811, and issued a decree on November 8, 1815. Article 1 of the latter provided that the chairs of public law would teach the principles of Bentham's legislation, those of constitutional law would teach from the works of

Constant [Henri Benjamin Constant de Rebecque (1767–1830)] or Lepage and those of international law would teach from the works of Vattel [Emmerich de Vattel, 1714–1767, Swiss jurist]. Article 2 provided that the rectors of the colleges and universities and the governors of the provinces would see that these laws were carried out.

Neither should I omit that, far from seeking the Chair of Public Law of San Bartolomé, I had not considered it because of the demands of my present occupation and because I felt there were others who were well qualified; I accepted the Chair only after the entreaties of friends and the request made by Your Excellency.

Preaching is a public function that cannot be exercised without the consent of the government. Nor can preaching exceed the limits established by law. No one can publicly convene, harangue, and make proclamations to the people without permission of the constituted authorities. No matter how sacred the place where the meeting is held, no matter how holy the purpose of the meeting, the government still has the supreme and irrevocable right of inspection in order to maintain public order and to determine that the exercise of sacred rights is not abused. The office of preacher has its restrictions and its responsibilities the same as any other public office. Its purpose is to explain the faith in simple terms and to recommend good habits. Whatever exceeds these two purposes is an abuse of privilege and a usurpation of governmental power deserving of punishment.

The preacher cannot voice his private opinions nor advocate as truth doctrines that are doubtful, or problematical or questionable. Much less can he censure or qualify government decrees and laws of the Republic, or incite the populace to disobedience; he is prohibited from calling persons heretics, excommunicating them, or condemning the education and rules of operation of respectable public institutions. Defamation and calumny are detestable crimes when committed by private persons;

they are subject to severe punishment. Defamation and calumny from the mouth of a priest, speaking before his congregation, from the Chair of the Holy Spirit, and in the refuge of the Sanctuary while discharging a public ministry and subject to the law, is not only a sacrilege, but a profanation of the temple, an insult to divinity itself. If the object of the defamation is the government or a leader of education or a magistrate appointed to the highest court, then the preacher, besides being a defamer, is a disturber of public peace and a rebel.

When congregations are behind closed doors, as they are during services, the government needs to be especially vigilant. Preachers who are enemies of the established order speak more boldly under such concealment; they are more certain that no one will report what they said to the authorities. They know how to snare timid and pious souls with the bait of vehemence, exaggerated illustrations, and other means of arousing fear. Although preachers should arouse the emotions of their listeners, practices of the kind I have mentioned are subject to abuses of which the history of the Church furnishes many examples. Services should not be held without the knowledge of the government; they should be conducted by virtuous and patriotic priests. Priests known to have fanatical ideas and doubtful intentions toward the government must be prohibited from preaching. Such prohibition applies especially to men like Doctor Margalló who indoctrinate their listeners with principles opposed to the government and its laws whose ultimate effect is to disturb the peace.

Although Your Excellency knows that many laws have been broken, I must cite some of the violations to support my case and, if this letter is published, for the education of the general public. A Royal Order of March 16, 1801, stated:

Some priests, lacking the spirit of charity that ought to infuse their sermons, have abused the Chair of the Holy Spirit by arousing their faithful flock with controversial ideas in order to depreciate the merits of their rivals. I encharge the bishops and provincials of the secular and regular clergy to prohibit their members from abusing their sacred ministry by speaking on controversial matters; this must be forbidden no matter how strongly the priest may feel about the subject. Priests must confine their exhortations to pointing out the path that leads to virtue and avoids vice. I command the tribunals and justices to be vigilant about these matters, to make what corrections their office permits, and to report violations to my Secretary of Grace and Justice.

When the French ambassador to Spain complained that a priest made offensive remarks in his sermon about the French government, the king, by Royal Order of June 14, 1799, instructed the Council [Secretariat of Grace and Justice] to confiscate the priest's license and to instruct the bishops that such abuses of the ministry must not recur.

Law 19, Title 12, Book I, of the *Recopilacion de Indias*,[1] provides for the following:

We order bishops and provincials to warn priests that their sermons must not include criticisms of the government or remarks calculated to arouse hatred for the government in any or all their listeners; let their remarks be confined to the doctrines which parishioners expect to hear. Especially must they refrain from public criticism of judicial officials; if they know of defects in justice, they should discuss these among themselves and seek corrections by authorized methods. We order our viceroys, governors, and *audiencias* to whom these violations become known to discuss the matter amicably with the bishops and provincials. If this proves ineffective, violators of this order must be sent to Spain.

The *cedula* of September 18, 1769, declared that love and respect for the government is an obligation and a matter of conscience which is required of all citizens by the fundamental laws of the State. It said that priests are therefore required to indoctrinate the people with these principles

---

[1] The legal code for colonial Spanish America.

whether by sermons, spiritual exercises, or devout acts. They must abstain on all public occasions and in private conversations from making critical and depreciatory comments about officials of the government; such comments arouse hatred for the government that may lead to such overt actions against it as constitute treason under Law 2, Title 1, Book 3, *Novísima Recopilación*.[2] The law just stated requires bishops and provincials to take into custody any priest who speaks against the State or government. This *cedula* was to be circulated among all clerical officials so that by knowledge of the law, the innocent might be protected and the guilty prosecuted.

Part 7 of Article 7 of the [Colombian] law of 1814 on ecclesiastical patronage says: The intendants will prevent ecclesiastics from dealing with matters belonging properly to the civil power and from violating the laws of the government. The intendants will require competent judges to apprehend and punish those who commit such violations; should this prove ineffective, the Executive Power will be notified.

This matter concerns Your Excellency since Articles 113, 114, 124, 125, and 126 of the Constitution [of 1821] and Articles 1 and 6 of the Law of Patronage, provide that criminals shall not go unpunished and that no one may disturb order nor intervene in what does not pertain to his office; that those delinquent in their official duties will be discharged or even arrested; that religious exercises cannot serve as opportunity for making disrespectful remarks about the government, and that preachers cannot indoctrinate parishioners with their own point of view.

These, among various others, are the just laws dealing with this matter. Your Excellency has used other similar provisions when the occasion warranted it such as the pastorals and decrees of the Archbishop

concerning factitious preachers. Doctor Margalló has mocked all the laws and continued his undertaking ever more boldly in spite of the government and the bishops. All moderate means have been exhausted; it is time to carry out the law in all its severity. I am appealing direct to Your Excellency because I am convinced that nothing less than your high authority can be effective.

With this object in mind, and because I consider the matter of major importance, allow me to make some additional comments about the ridiculous criticisms that this seditious priest has made of the writings of Bentham and other publicists, and about his persistent attacks on the system of education — that primary need of all good government and the basis for a republic. Allow me also to comment on the character and conduct of this man during the Revolution. My comments will prove the necessity for the provisions adopted by the government, and will remove the doubts of any person who holds them unwarranted.

Doctor Margalló bases his condemnation of the work of Bentham on the bull of the *cena*;[3] this bull, attributed by some to Martin V [1417–1435] and by others to Boniface VIII [1294–1303], was ordered by Paul III [1534–1549] to be published annually on Holy Thursday; it has been in existence, then, for 200 years before Bentham was born or his works were published. The bull, therefore, prophetically bans his works for its authors could not know whether Bentham's works were good or bad. On such a flimsy basis as this absurd theologians found their doctrines. They are ignorant of even the precepts of Jesus Christ on excommunication and still they dogmatize principles long ago discredited in the whole Catholic world. And what was the famous bull *In coena Domini*? It was an act of rebellion against the sovereignty of nations and the Catholic Church itself. Its content convinces us of

---

2 *Novísima Recopilación de las Leyes de España* (1805), compiled by Juan de la Reguera y Valdelomar. That the Indies were to be governed by the laws of Spain, rather than by their own code, was indicative of the centralist trend in government.

3 Literally supper; its meaning here is the Last Supper, which was held on Thursday.

this. It excommunicates heretics, their supporters, and those who read their books; according to this bull we must not read English, North American, or even the majority of European works. We must ban the work of Grotius, Pufendorf, Heineccius, Wolff, Watel, and Winio[4] because they are heretics; if we read them we shall be excommunicated. Persons would thus be excommunicated who in any way intervene in church affairs whether by granting privileges or exacting fines; judges, members of *audiencias*, chancelleries, and councils would be included. Also included would be the legal representatives of towns who deal with ecclesiastical matters, and all those who have written or published, or will write or publish edicts, regulations, and pragmatics by which ecclesiastical liberties or the rights of the Pope and the Holy See may in any way be infringed.

*   *   *

These are the senseless excommunications covered by the notorious bull *In coena Domini*. After appreciating what ridiculous inferences can be drawn from this bull, who would not be astonished that anyone in Colombia would dare to use this bull to defame the government, to incite people to disobedience of the law, and to disturb the peace? The bull is one of many that serve as a horrible example of the abuse of spiritual power that formerly was practiced; this power was used to disturb the peace of nations and to despoil the government of its rights. All the Catholic monarchs and Catholic governments rejected the bull. Even the hypocritical Philip II of Spain banned it from his dominions; nor was it ever accepted in Spain or in America. The wise Ganganell[i],[5] honor and glory of the Chair of St. Peter, poisoned by a fanatic inspired by the papacy, suppressed its publication. In short, to try to enforce observance of this

lawless bull would be tantamount to inciting rebellion.

And what is the source of this sudden attack on the works of Bentham? Shameful ignorance, stupid fanaticism, and mean prejudice. For many years Bentham's works have been known, cited, copied, and venerated by various national writers and even writers under the Bourbon monarchy and the infamous Inquisition. *Practical criminal de España* [Spanish Criminal Law] by Marcos Gutiérrez is in most libraries and has been in the hands of most jurists. After adopting and explaining the doctrines of Bentham, Gutiérrez wrote a eulogy to Bentham which he inserted at the end of the first volume. The Bourbon monarchy had Bentham's treatises on legislation translated for use in education; the work circulated freely in spite of the fact that the Catholic religion was the only faith permitted. Bentham has been congratulated for his excellent works by the Portuguese court, the leading literary men of France and Spain, the government of Switzerland, the government and statesmen of the United States, the members of the English House of Commons, and even the late Alexander [Alexander I (1801–1825)] of Russia. Bentham has been asked by statesmen or governments of three nations to draft a code of laws; few if any scholars have received so much homage from the learned societies of Europe and America and from the outstanding men of the civilized world. As his Spanish translator justifiably says:

The more the doctrines of Bentham are studied, the better they are appreciated. These doctrines are now being applied to modern legislation, which affords Bentham a pleasure that comes to few scholars in their lifetimes. By this use of his doctrines, the present generation has already become Bentham's posterity. To be appreciated the more it is studied is a characteristic of all useful and profound works. At first made weary by reading this work, the reader ultimately becomes fascinated with it.

During the last, ominous years of the Bourbon government, Bentham's treatises

---

[4] Identifiable are Hugo Grotius (1583–1645), Dutch publicist; the German jurists Samuel Pufendorf (1632–1694), and Johann Gottlieb Heineccius (1681–1741); and the German philosopher, Christian Wolff (1679–1754).

[5] Pope Clement XIV (1769–1774).

on legislation were secretly read and meditated upon by Camilo Torres, Camacho, Pombo,[6] and other famous martyrs and founders of independence. His doctrines were printed in *La Bagatela,* which General Nariño[7] published in the early years of the Republic; the leading senators and representatives frequently cited them in the halls of Congress. Various laws have been drawn up in accordance with their principles. And what patriotic, literate Colombian does not try to acquire and study Bentham's works? No aspect of legislation has been ignored by this intellectual giant; he has shown wisdom and profundity in his analysis of all aspects. All his works are classics; some are unique of their kind. He has been the first man to place legislation on a scientific basis. Before him, we had Montesquieu, Beccaria, and Filangieri.[8] Although the works of these men were valuable, they were imperfect. The authors left important matters untouched. It was reserved for this creative genius to develop all branches of legislation fruitfully, to classify the laws, to relate underlying principles to each other, and to deduce from them, all rights, duties, and truths.

His works on civil and criminal law, which the government has wisely ordered to be taught, and which have been the object of Doctor Margalló's attacks, constitute a body of doctrine unequalled in scope by any other work that I know of. It is the first orderly treatment that we have of penal science, and the only work in which civil laws rest on rational principles. These works are an excellent course in the logic of law, and in the elemental truths about society; moreover they contain valuable ideas about political economy. From them one can see the basis for morals and for public, private, and international law — a basis that is purer and conforms more closely to Christian principles.[9] One learns more from this single work of Bentham than from thousands of other works. As the author himself says, inventions and methods are not found in books of law but in works dealing with metaphysics, physics, natural history, and medicine. One will find little in Tribonian, Coccey, Blackstone, Vattel, Pothier, Domat; much more useful are the works of Hume, Helvetius, Linneas, Bergman, and Cullen.[10] Therefore not only is there nothing pernicious in teaching the principles of Bentham's legislation, but his works are more suitable than any others if one does not want youth to waste their time in learning vague and mistaken ideas that are later difficult to modify or forget. Although there are excellent authors among other publicists, in general they only repeat each other and treat doctrines that are well known and easily acquired from many writers. One finds in Bentham's works what is either treated confusingly elsewhere or is neglected; he uses a better method of classification, new sources, and new principles. He lights a path that one can confidently follow.

Doctor Margalló admits that he has never read Bentham's works; one believes it for he furnishes abundant evidence. In spite of this, he condemns Benthamite doctrines. Is this not where fanaticism always leads — to this last stage of delirium? Is not the conduct of this false apostle like that of the caliph who burned the library at Alexandria because its books either agreed with the Koran and were therefore

---

[6] Camilo Torres, Joaquín Camacho, and Miguel Pombo were shot as traitors by the Spanish in 1816.

[7] Antonio Nariño (1765–1823), independence leader who translated *The Declaration of the Rights of Man.*

[8] The last two names refer to the Italian publicist Cesare Benesana Beccaria (1738–1794), and to Gaetano Filangieri (1752–1788), Italian lawyer.

[9] Although Azuero omitted his basis for comparison, what he probably had in mind was the pessimistic view of human nature assumed by traditional Christianity contrasted with the optimistic view of the Enlightenment.

[10] The less well-known persons identifiable are: Tribonian, 5th-century jurist of Justinian; Sir William Blackstone (1723–1780), English jurist; the French jurists Robert Joseph Pothier (1699–1772); Jean Domat (1625–1696); the Swedish naturalist, Tobern Olof Bergman (1735–1784); and the Scottish physician, William Cullen (1710–1790).

useless, or disagreed with it and were therefore dangerous? It is well known that no publicist is as cautious as Bentham is in advocating adoption of his doctrines. He wrote his works for all governments and all faiths; he attacks neither. He addresses himself to all governments and faiths in order that they may perfect themselves by reform. He ridicules no belief; unlike books that can be properly called dangerous, his books attack neither the basis for beliefs nor their dogmas. On the contrary, he establishes four sanctions — natural, religious, political, and moral — that the legislator should respect. In his hands all four can be a powerful instrument for promotion of the public welfare. Far from impugning the Catholic faith, Bentham supports it as indispensable for happiness. Such is the man who is accused of impiety and heresy by a preacher whose information is based on rumor and hearsay! Bentham rests his system of laws on the principle of the general happiness. Ignorant men have criticized this enlightened and well-proved principle. And what will they say when they find out that the Christian faith rests on it, and that it is the soul of evangelical morals? Hear the truth from the mouth of a respected father of the Church. San Juan Crisóstomo[11] says: The rule of Christianity, its essence, the apex of the Catholic edifice, is: be concerned for the public happiness. Bentham teaches that happiness is pleasure, or the cause of pleasure; pain is evil or the cause of evil. Jesus himself taught this when He said that My yoke is easy; He meant that the sacrifices required by religion cause more pleasure than pain. To analyze all the pleasures and pains attendant to an action, to prefer what produces the most happiness, to select from all the goods or pleasures the greatest and most satisfying, and to reject those that are smaller or only apparently pleasurable — this in short is the doctrine of Jeremy Bentham. Only malignity and prejudice could discount the evidence supporting this principle. In con-

demning rigorous asceticism he is in agreement with the Catholic Church which has condemned the Flagellants, Molinistas,[12] Iluminados [Illuminati] and other extremist sects. I fear that Doctor Margalló and some of his fanatical proselytes are themselves liable to be condemned by the church, which justly prohibits practices that make humans useless to themselves and to society.

It must not be supposed however that I support all Bentham's ideas as if his work were sacred. Any man willing to use his mind does not bow before the authority of any writer. What writer has not made errors? The work of an author can be the basis for teaching. This does not mean that either the teachers or the pupils must accept all of it; nor should its excellent principles be rejected merely because it contains defects. Let the slave of fanaticism and superstition revere as dogma the bad books that have been his sole nourishment. Let him not suffer the slightest doubt nor tolerate the smallest contradiction. Does Doctor Margalló fear that Bentham might discuss religion? Does he fear that he might discover the vices, insanities, uncurbed ambitions, and evils that comprise fanaticism? His fears are vain. One could assure him that there is more danger in the ecclesiastical annals of Cardinal Baronio, in the history and clerical discourses of Abbot Fleury, in the writings of San Pedro Damiano, San Bernardo, Cardinal Pedro de Ally, Nicolás de Clemanjis, Alvaro Pelagio, Claudio Espenceo,[13] and many other respected Catholic writers. He should preach against the reading of these books; they vividly portray the crimes of hypocrisy, ambition, and fanaticism. Perhaps he wishes to keep the people in complete ignorance of them.

If we were to accept the strange ideas of Doctor Margalló, I do not know what

---

[11] St. John Chrysostom (345–407), Greek Christian priest.

[12] Followers of Miguel de Molinos (c. 1640–1697), Spanish mystic condemned to life imprisonment by the Inquisition at Rome.

[13] The references are to the Italian church historian, Caesar Barenius (1538–1607); the Italian cleric, St. Pietro Damiani (c. 1007–1072); the French writers, Mateo Nicolas de Poillevillain de

books could be used to teach public law. There is no publicist of stature whose work does not contain maxims directly opposite to those professed by this priest. He has asserted that doctrines taught in the Colegio of El Rosario are purer than those taught in San Bartolomé; but in the former, lessons have been given from *The Spirit of the Laws* by Montesquieu, and it would not be difficult to show that this author engages in more invective against religion than can be found in all Bentham's works. In that *colegio,* teachers have expounded on the *Social Contract* by Rousseau. How Rousseau treats religion is well known. Teachers of that *colegio* have read and explained the *Rights of People* by Vatel who is a strict Protestant and often attacks dogmas and orthodox practices of the [Roman Catholic] Church. At present, they are teaching from the *Science of Law* by Lepage; this work also contains various chapters on religion and vigorously argues for religious tolerance, which Doctor Margalló detests and regards as heresy. These works, which I certainly do not censure, indicate how prejudiced one is who limits his criticism to me and the Colegio de San Bartolomé. Is this persecution directed at ideas or persons? If directed at ideas, why has he not attacked the teaching of other authors? Doctor Margalló displayed shameful ignorance and contradicted himself when he exhorted his listeners in the Church of the Third Order to abandon the teachings of Bentham and transfer to the Colegio of El Rosario to study the works of Lepage. This is the position in which he finds himself because he has attacked what he has not read, and has announced his personal opinions rather than confined his remarks to Christian morality.

Let us not be deceived. If we were subject to the dogmatic opinions of these enemies of the Enlightenment, there would be no books available for teaching. Out of

stupidity, they would condemn liberty as heresy, the Republic as impious, independence as rebellion, and tolerance as an assault on the faith. To confine the Church to spiritual matters, in their view, is to create a schism between Church and State. They would consign all publicists who advocate this to the flames. But who would not support the sacred rights of man? Who would not oppose the temporal power of the Pope? Who would not impugn ultramontane doctrines? Among the books treating Church-State policy, which have been published with the approval of the Spanish Inquisition, I am aware only of those of Villadiego and Bobadilla.[14] If we are to put in the hands of youth only the works of intolerant and ultramontane Catholics, then we must burn the works of Cicero, Virgil, Tito Livio, Cornelio Nepos, Fedro[15] — all the writers of Latin civilization because the authors were Gentiles. We must also burn our Constitution and laws because they contain many articles borrowed from the heretical laws of England and the United States, and from doctrines of Deists, Protestants, and the Intramontanes[16] of France. This would be much to the liking of Doctor Margalló, that eternal enemy of our revolution and our liberties. To malign us and to arouse hatred for our holy cause, he said in the church of Santa Gertrudis that even boys would soon be saying to their mothers: long live the Republic and death to Religion.

* * *

Margalló's hatred has not been confined to political institutions and the progress of our Republic but has been extended even

---

Clemangis (c. 1360–c. 1437) and Claude Fleury (1640–1732); the famous St. Bernard of Clairvaux (1090–1153) and the French theologian Claude D'Espence (1511–1571); and the famous early exponent of free will, the British monk, Pelagius (c. 360–c. 420). Ally is not identifiable.

14 The 16th-century Spanish jurisconsult, Alonso Villadiego Vascuñana y Montoya, and Nicolás de Bobadilla (1510–1590), a founder of the Jesuit order.

15 The last three names refer to Titus Livius (Livy) (59 B.C.–A.D. 17), the Roman historian Cornelius Nepos (c. 99 B.C.–24 B.C.), and, presumably, the Greek Epicurean philosopher, Fedro (?–A.D. 70).

16 Those holding that the national government need not obey decisions of the Pope, whose residence was ultramontane, that is, across the Alps, from France.

to our writers. He has never read our Constitution and our laws; what he knows of the official actions of our officials rests on the distorted account of his lackeys and informers. He hates our newspapers and official pronouncements and considers it a sin to read them. In spite of the abolishing of the Inquisition and the restoration to Colombia of precious freedom of expression, he maintains respect for its ridiculous restrictions and would apply them even to what the government releases to the press. His principles and conduct contradict Holy Gospel, for the Gospel reveals the equality of man, but this priest loves the old servility. The basis of religion is love; but Doctor Margalló teaches hatred, persecution, and terror. It would seem that Jesus Christ had him in mind when he said: "Beware of false prophets wearing sheep's clothing; inside, they are ravenous wolves." Compare this priest's deeds with what St. Paul says of charity: "Charity is patient; it is kind; it is not envious; it works not hastily, and is not puffed up; it is not ambitious; it does not seek its own advantage, is not moved to anger, does not think evil; it enjoys not iniquity but truth. It endures all things, believes all things, hopes all things, suffers all things." Let Doctor Margalló be compared with this picture by the Apostle.

*   *   *

There is grave risk in abandoning to this devout incendiary the direction of the consciences of a people among whom are not only many simple and innocent souls but many pious and incautious women. Still less should he be permitted to hold weeklong meetings under the pretext of holding spiritual exercises. For these reasons the secret meetings of Priscillian in the 4th century were prohibited, as were the meetings of the Society of Jesus in the present one. The Church itself, entrusted by Jesus Christ to conserve pure and holy customs, is the one which gives us these sane lessons; let them guide our conduct.

Now I must complete this picture. I have tried to show the harm that has been done by Doctor Margalló's seditious preaching during the last Lenten period. I have indicated the laws that he has violated, and have shown that his character, his principles, and his deeds are opposed to the glorious cause of Colombia and destructive of the public happiness. I have pointed out the danger that surrounds us as a result of his work. I have duly defended the official policy for education and I have vindicated myself of the defamatory charges made against my teachings. If I have been too lengthy, I am excused by the importance of these matters to my country. In Colombia, all criminals, all lawbreakers, must feel the rod of justice. Miserable men are sent to *presidios* or are executed for minor crimes. Leading statesmen, generals who have saved the country, suffer severe penalties. The law judges all people alike for by them it was fashioned. Can a rebel, an obstinate enemy of our liberties, be granted special immunity? Absolutely not. And in conclusion, I request that Your Excellency:

1. Order the Secretary of the Interior or the Intendant of the Department to gather evidence and the statements of witnesses about what took place in the churches of the Third Order, Santa Gertrudis, and San Bartolomé.

2. Request the Vicar-General to recall Doctor Margalló's licenses to confess and preach.

3. Order the Superior Court of Justice to prosecute Doctor Margalló, imposing on him, as the law demands, the sentence of banishment from the country.

4. Order that the names of all priests preaching or conducting spiritual exercises be furnished the Intendant, or at least the Vicar-General, in order that those suspected of disturbing the public peace or abusing their privilege in any way, can be prohibited from carrying out these functions.

5. Instruct congress to write a new law that deals more specifically with such abuses committed in the ministry of preaching and provides a more severe punishment for the violation of the law.

Jesus Christ or Jeremy Bentham

JOSÉ MANUEL GROOT

Of Dutch ancestry, José Manuel Groot (1800–1878) was born and died in Bogotá, where he was for many years a doughty champion of Catholic conservatism against the rising tide of secularism and liberalism. An eye-witness to many civil wars in Colombia, his years of research in the national archives and his some dozen publications were testimony to a determination, inspired by what he had seen, to defend his cause by the pen. The titles of some of his works suggest the ground where he took his stand: *The Missionaries of Heresy, or a Defense of the Catholic Dogmas* (1853); *An Analytical Refutation of the Book of Mons. Renan* (1865); *Ecclesiastical and Civil History of New Granada,* 5 vols. (1869), which was his greatest work; and *God and Country* (1894). The selection that follows is taken from the ecclesiastical history.

THE Vice-President and his ministry were not satisfied that in Colombia one could do whatever he wished in the matter of religion without running any risk of censure from Church or State. On November 8, 1825, they issued a decree requiring that Bentham's legislation must be taught in all *colegios.* This was the worst blow ever suffered by the faith. Bentham's ideas are worse than those found in Freemasonry, those advocated by the Bible Society, or those contained in immoral books imported from abroad. The ideas in these last-mentioned sources are only tares among the wheat, which might choke its growth. But Bentham's legislation could root up the good seed and sow the bad. A man who is a Protestant, a Jew, or a Mohammedan can show love for his fellow man, and can be generous and patriotic; and, if he finally goes to the devil, at least he has been of benefit to mundane society. But a Benthamist, a disciple of sensualism, is devoid of conscience or concern for God, fellow man, or country. His only concern is his ego; he thinks there is nothing beyond death. Consequently, his actions are guided by no moral principle and have no other purpose than to experience pleasurable sensations. If there ever were a society of such creatures, it is impossible to see how it could exist since each member's morality is based on his own appetites and comfort.

Needless to say, the present Benthamists have escaped part of the evil inherent in their system because they are living in a society formed by very different morals and because they themselves received a spiritual education in primary school which checks their development along purely Benthamist lines. It could be said of them what Mr. Augusto Nicolás [Auguste Nicolas (1807–1888)] said of the relation of Protestants to Protestantism:

Protestantism has not caused all the evil in society which, by its theory, it is capable of, because Protestants are better than Protestantism and the realization of Protestantism depends on the transmission from generation to generation of a sentiment different from that in which the first Protestants were born and raised. As the sects draw farther and farther

From José Manuel Groot, *Historia eclesiástica y civil de Nueva Granada,* 5 vols. (2nd ed.; Bogotá 1889–93), V, pp. 61–64, 127–141, 200–215.

away from their origins, however, they move closer and closer to skepticism and approach atheism and materialism.

The first Benthamists who emerge from a Catholic society can do little harm, for it is against their reason and will to be pure Benthamists. But this system is worse than Protestantism, because it kills in the germ the spiritualist principle that the other conserves. Like a plant surrounded by nettles, spiritualism will soon die out in a nation that adopts Benthamism as its guide for public education; in two or three generations the spiritual sense will have been extinguished in the heart of men shaped under the influence of utilitarian materialism. By substituting for sane morals those of sensualism, and by permitting them to be transmitted from father to son, a society doing this will soon have — as Voltaire predicted for any society accepting this philosophy — a *beautiful quarrel*.

Señor Restrepo[1] says that this decree alarmed many parents with thin consciences. But it is not necessary to have a thin conscience to be alarmed by it. From the principle of self-interest, which is the basis of Bentham's system, youth have drawn erroneous conclusions that are prejudicial to their morals. They discovered this only by experience since "this could not be foreseen as Bentham's work was not well known." This excuse of the Secretary [Restrepo] who authorized the decree, seems to be evidence that we now have fanatics of another kind than those who not long ago formed the [Masonic] lodges. Only foolhardiness and fanaticism could have inspired a decree ordering the teaching of law in the *colegios* from a book containing such depraved ideas of morality. Its morals are diametrically opposed to those of the Gospel which the world knows to be the primary moral law. The Secretary dismisses the matter with the excuse that the work still was not well known. But this puts him in a worse position. Why designate as a

text for youth a work whose moral principles are not well known? Could this be done by a ministry of enlightened men? And was not Bentham's ten-volume treatise on legislation translated by Salas and circulated in eight volumes in Bogotá before 1824? And was it not taught in the *colegio* of San Bartolomé long before the issuance of this decree? General Santander has zealously studied this legislation; the work was always at his elbow and he never stopped reading it except to write letters or sign documents. But why say more on this point? The private advisers of General Santander, like Doctor Azuero, who defend Bentham's teaching consider it well known by Colombians and the best book ever written.

*   *   *

This lamentable decree has caused some youth to flee from the schools and caused others not to enroll in them. Some parents would rather have their sons possess good morals than to have them attracted by the glitter of a career that cannot be pursued except by sacrificing what is much more valuable. Their protests are known to the government by direct presentations and through the press. But another text could not be substituted, which makes it clear that it was not so much instruction in law as indoctrination in sensualism and materialism that was desired.

*   *   *

In the midst of many disturbances and problems, says Señor Restrepo, the Executive Power under General Santander did not lose sight of reforms that would benefit society and educate the people. On October 3, [1826], the Vice-President issued a decree for a general plan of studies authorized by a legislative act of March 18 of the same year. This plan was prepared by a committee of *chosen* men headed by the Secretary of the Interior [Restrepo]. The plan outlined a uniform organization for primary and secondary schools and universities, which was supposed to improve education

[1] José Manuel Restrepo (1781–1863), a statesman and historian.

and extend it throughout the Republic. Restrepo wrote:

It is true that the new plan contained some serious defects, one of which was that it authorized certain books to be used. This did not allow for the continuous progress then being made in the arts and sciences. But this could be changed and the entire plan could be improved in other ways. There was much opposition to establishment of the plan for it attacked old customs and habits; however, the government knew how to overcome this by working carefully but firmly. The plan was in effect for some years and, as a result, much progress was made in general education.

What handicaps former members of the government are under when they try to be historians! Señor Restrepo, Secretary of the Interior, head of the committee of *chosen ones* who made the plan, authorized it by his signature but, as historian, confesses to its defects and at the same time tries to avoid placing the government in a bad light. How difficult it is for him to get over this obstacle in the road! All of us have lived through our time of errors. Let us not deceive ourselves. We see more clearly now and if we must judge the past, it is best to begin with our errors. In this way we can reach our goals of the future by a straight route and with a firm step.

Señor Restrepo is embarrassed by this subject. Why? Because the great evil, in our opinion the evil of evils, to be charged against the administration of General Santander is the system of university studies for the propagation of materialism and atheism, which obliged all Colombians who desire this level of education to become infected with the pestilential doctrine of Tracy and Bentham. Imagine the anguish this has caused their parents! . . .

What impeded the progress of enlightened knowledge in Colombia was the designation by the government of certain authors for the study of philosophy and law. Although there were undesirable texts in other subjects, none were so prejudicial to society as these; they undermined the moral basis of society, and made the soul and mind, both inspirations of God, mere organic mechanisms; they denied the existence of natural law, of conscience, of God, and of a future life. In short, they did not recognize a spiritual order.

To avoid so great an evil as this, many parents preferred to leave their sons in ignorance rather than see them perverted. Their decision was wise. They preferred a healthy ignorance to a perverted wisdom, having in mind the words of Jesus Christ: "What shall it profit a man if he shall gain the whole world and lose his own soul?" But what wise men were graduated from these *colegios*? The results were obvious; there were no mathematicians, or physicists. There were only scientific charlatans and political demagogues. Foolishly proud, they made themselves ridiculous by imitating whatever was done in France and the United States.

As Señor Restrepo wrote, there was much opposition to the establishment of the new system of studies. Yes, for good reason. The immediate results on the morality of youth had been unfortunate. These results were visible within two years — a year since the Executive signed the decree of November 8 [1825] that ordered the sensualism of Bentham to be taught. From that date until October 3, when the *chosen ones* published their plan, there were pleas to revoke these teachings and protests against them, and even verbal conflicts between the *chosen ones* and those who protested, like the complaint of Doctor Vicente Azuero against Doctor Margalló. Nevertheless, the Executive ruled in favor of the decision of the *chosen ones* against that of the people; in this way there took place in Colombia what the Gospel says: "Many are called but few are chosen." For in the Republic, the people are called to make the law but it is *the chosen* who actually hand it down against the will of the people. And, as Señor Restrepo says, there was much opposition to the establishment of the plan of studies because it attacked old customs and habits. In what sense were old customs and habits attacked? Merely in that Bentham and Tracy[2] taught materialism and destroyed the basis of the Christian, Apostolic, Roman religion that was protected by a law of the very government which permitted its destruction. Then these habits and customs of which Señor Restrepo spoke must be belief in God, in the soul, and in the rewards and punishments of a future life. . . .

We shall now consider certain articles of the plan of studies and comment on them. . . . Article 157. Ideology or metaphysics, general grammar, and logic. A professor will teach these branches which will include what is useful under metaphysics. The *Ideology* of Destutt de Tracy will be read, and the professor can also consult Condillac's[3] works on logic, and on the origin of human knowledge and sensations, as well as those of other authors. . . . Now, we have all students of philosophy at the door of the halls of law; these doors will not open unless they carry the passport of Destutt de Tracy. All of them carry it, of course; all of them know that to feel is to think; therefore horses think because they feel. As a result, we are like horses except that we have a different shape. But what about human reason? It is of no importance; man learns through his senses. . . . After lessons in this fine philosophy the students are prepared for their first lesson from Bentham which says: "Nature has placed man under the rule of pleasure and pain; these sensations give rise to all our ideas." And brutes are also placed by nature under the rule of pleasure and pain; to eat gives them pleasure and to be wounded gives them pain. Doubtless, they too have ideas.

Our only object is to seek pleasure and avoid pain.[4] These eternal and irresistible feelings should be our main study. The principle of utility organizes everything under these two motives; utility is the first link in his chain of teachings. Evil is pain, grief, or their cause. Good is pleasure or the cause of pleasure. These words, pain and pleasure are to be taken in their ordinary signification; there is no need to invent special definitions in order to exclude certain pleasures or to deny the existence of certain pains. Pain and pleasure is what all of us feel — the farmer, the prince, the ignorant, the wise, and the pig. Virtue is not a good except when it causes pleasure; vice is not an evil except when it causes pain. Thus, in the catalog of virtues (like the Ten Commandments), if you find a virtue that produces more pain than pleasure, erase it and write it in the catalog of vices; and, in the catalog of vices (like that of the Seven Mortal Sins) if you find one that innocently produces pleasure, erase it, and write it in the catalog of virtues.

The logic of utility [the capacity of any object or action to produce pleasure or happiness] consists in classifying all sensations as either pains or pleasures. By a process of moral calculus the elements — pleasures and pains — are graded by intensity, duration, certainty, proximity, fertility, and purity. This last word means that there must be no possibility of the pleasure producing pain. Adding up the pleasures and the pains [of a contemplated action], one makes a comparison; the balance determines what action to take. By this knowledge, each person calculates his own happiness. This is as it should be for man would be irrational if he did not make this judgment; the man that does not determine what is suitable for him is less than a child — he is an idiot. The rules of this calculus are the same as for any other kind of calculation except that we may after consulting the thermometer of our fancies, alter the value of the figures. Craving to do some evil act, we can increase the value of the pleasure and lower the value of the pain in accordance with the intensity of our desire. You will tell us, perhaps, that utility is nothing more than Epicureanism and that the evil influence of

[2] The French philosopher Antoine Claude Destutt Tracy (1754–1836).

[3] Étienne Bonnot de Condillac (1715–1780).

[4] Groot proceeds to blend a paraphrasing of Bentham with his own commentary in such a way that it is difficult to distinguish between them.

that doctrine on customs is well known. But the analogy is inexact. Although it is true that Epicurus [341–270 B.C.] knew the true source of morals, to suppose that his doctrine corrupted him is to suppose that happiness can be the enemy of happiness. It is said that man has a thing inside him that tells him what is good and what is bad, and that thing is called conscience. There is no such thing as conscience; like natural law and natural rights, it is a fiction. The only natural law is that composed of the sensations of pain and pleasure. . . .

Although hardly a month had passed since approval of the study plan, it already began to bear fruit because its authors were teaching in the Colegio de San Bartolomé by arrangement of Vice-President Santander. In the *Bandera Tricolor* an article appeared, probably written by Doctor Vicente Azuero, professor of law, describing the mastery of Benthamite doctrines by the students of the *colegio*. According to this article, Colombia had left Europe behind:

Today for the first time there was presented in Colombia expositions of the universal principles of morality and legislation. But how strange! In Europe, the rudiments of this science are just beginning to be studied.

What he means is that the works of Bentham were still not being studied in Europe. This strikes Doctor Azuero as strange because he thinks knowledge and Bentham are synonymous. These *chosen ones* might as well burn all other books, including the Gospel, because they have been made useless by the works of Bentham. But the doctor is right in saying that Bentham's works have not been studied in Europe because not only did European universities refuse to adopt them, but they were impugned by many learned publicists and moralists; in some cities the works of Bentham were even banned. Only the Russian Tzar adopted them. A great honor for Bentham!

*   *   *

By the middle of [1827] public protest against the teachings of Bentham was general. Protests poured in to the Vice-President from all provinces asking that another work be substituted for that of Bentham. General Santander and Doctor Vicente Azuero had been writing articles in the *Gaceta* which did not so much discuss Bentham's doctrines as charge that his critics were ignorant, fanatical, and supporters of *godismo*. But the general clamor induced the Vice-President to take some action. One would think that he might select a new textbook, since the study plan calls for the provisional designation of texts. But no! The use of the word provisional was merely deception. Bentham was the soul of the program of studies; to remove the soul would kill the program. The Vice-President asked for a report by the Committee of Studies which was composed of Doctor Azuero, Doctor Vergara,[5] and Señor Restrepo. The majority opinion, which excepted Señor Restrepo, stated that professors could continue to teach from Bentham but should warn their students that his works contained some things that should not be followed.

To teach Bentham's legislation without teaching what is evil was like trying to teach the astronomical system of Copernicus without teaching that the earth moved around the sun. It is obvious that the essence of Bentham's system is individual pleasure; the insistence of his followers that its essence is the happiness of society cannot alter this truth. On this matter, Bentham himself is clear and precise; one need quote only a single instance of proof. On theft, he says: "If a man, for example, steals public moneys he enriches himself but impoverishes no one because the harm done to all of society is insignificant."

In this way Bentham balances the pleasure of the thief against the pain (loss), not of the state or society, but of each individual. The thief has harmed no one, he says; but he has increased the sum of his own happiness, or the means to happiness. Thus the public interest counts for nothing

[5] Estanislao Vergara (1790–1854), Colombian jurisconsult.

when compared with individual interest; there is no harm to society in the theft of public income. Actually the principle is immoral rather than moral. It authorizes thieves to rob the State and the poor to rob the rich on the ground that the rich are not made poor as a result, and the thieves have met their needs.

It is necessary to examine the utilitarian principle a little further in order to appreciate why the government was asked to suppress the study of Bentham and what evil was done by the government's support of it. . . .

The principle of egoism could not be stated more clearly than Bentham has stated it. This principle is the basis of all our actions, according to Bentham, because it alone guides all our decisions. There is no mention here of generous and disinterested actions, of conscience, of deep feeling. All these are explained in the arbitrary terms of antipathies and sympathies. Give illustrations to a Benthamist of self-denial, generosity, the torture of a martyr, the austere life of an anchorite or penitent, the sacrificial life of one who has renounced all life's comforts to serve the poor and sick. He will hear you out, calmly, then will reply: "All this was done to win glory, to enjoy eternal happiness. Your examples illustrate the principle of utility, but by misguided actions."

*   *   *

Let us suppose that utilitarianism has spread throughout the country; even coal miners and bargemen know the moral arithmetic of sensualism. A canoe carrying a chest with 4,000 pesos in it sinks in the Magdalena river. The owner escapes with his life but with nothing else. News of the disaster is widely known, but all efforts to find the money fail. Then a poor man with a family finds the canoe with the money down river, caught in a drift; he waits until nightfall, then takes the money which he knows has been the object of a search. Does this man follow Christian morals? If he does, he will turn the money over to its possessor without debating his self-interest.

Any calculation made should he be tempted would be: God sees me; God will judge me; God orders me to hand the money over to its owner. But the man is a Benthamist. He takes two gourd cups and a little corn to make his calculations with because he knows moral but not ordinary arithmetic. He is going to determine the difference between good and evil, between profit and loss.

First, he says to himself that no one saw him recover the chest from the river, bury the money, and throw the chest back into the river. He can use the money to much advantage. Seeing no pain to himself on these accounts, he empties the corn from the cup which he calls the evil side, and fills the cup on the good side. He has the money, there is no fear of being discovered, he is rich for his class, and can support his family for the rest of his life without plying up and down the river in his boat. Next he balances this cup of good with another; that of delivering the money to its owner. He will reward me, he thinks. But a part is less than the whole and my good will be greater if I have all the money. He next calculates the pleasure he would feel at being considered an honest man. But, he calculates, what profit do I get out of being considered honest? I should be granted credit. And why do I want credit? To increase the volume of my trade? And why do I want to increase my trade? To make more money and live comfortably. Then I must conclude that I have reached this goal by a shorter road if I keep the money because according to my master of moral arithmetic, I have a right to keep it because right is the same thing as direct; good acts are those which lead men to happiness by the most direct and secure road; good acts, then, are direct actions, and since the act of keeping the money is the shortest road to becoming rich, which is in what my happiness consists, and since I am the judge of what my happiness is, I am morally correct in keeping the money. But I have one more calculation to make. I must balance my pleasure in being rich against the pain that the one who has lost the money will suffer; to judge this I follow the principle of utility which advises me to follow my own interest, not that of someone else. What, then, is the pain that the loser will suffer? To be poor himself if I do not give him his money? But I should suffer this pain if I gave him the money. The question, then, is reduced to one of us suffering the pain of poverty. Since the principle of utility orders me to prefer my own interest, and since I am the only judge of it, I shall keep the money. I have taken the shortest road away from poverty which proves that sensualist morals contain wisdom and truth. Ah, but I forgot one point! Beside being short, the road must be safe. How can I make the road secure, that is, make certain no one will discover that I have found the money? The answer lies in following closely the rule of the art of concealment which is part of sensualist morals. Therefore I shall not spend a penny the first year. After that the loss will be forgotten by the public. Then I shall begin with tiny investments in commerce and will pay my debts on time. In this way it will seem that I am making small profits; then I shall spend a little more money than before, gradually increasing the amount so that it will seem to be the profits from my business. Finally I shall have reached the point where no one can suspect the source of my income. All I need exercise is a little patience.

What he have here is a typical case reasoned out by the principles of moral arithmetic set forth by Bentham. And what would we say if in spite of all this manipulation of two gourds it turned out that the money brought evil to the man? Bentham would say what Don Quijote said when he was beaten by a page of the Toledan merchants: "The beating was not for any fault of mine but for that of my horse's." That is, the evil was not because of moral arithmetic but as a result of an error of the calculator and since the morality of actions should be judged by what profit the doer of them gained, their morality or immorality depends on one's skill in concealing crimes.

Whenever Bentham's law fails a person it is because he was a poor calculator, or a poor concealer; the only crime under utilitarianism is that of being a bad calculator. One is punished for lacking the talents of a successful rogue.

Bentham qualifies his egoistical system by stating that three things are necessary to make it effective and to make it work equally for all persons. Firstly, to define utility exactly so that all persons understand its meaning; secondly, to exclude all principles in conflict with it; thirdly, to work out the formulas of moral arithmetic. In spite of his unmistakeable emphasis upon self-interest, Bentham wishes to harmonize his system with the utility of society, or the public interest. To achieve this reconciliation of individual and public interest, he visualizes a judiciary to whom conflicts of interest could be referred; the judiciary is authorized by a pact among individuals, but even Rousseau tells us more about how such a pact might have originated than Bentham tells us.

As the result of an analysis of Bentham's doctrine, Mons. Jouffroy[6] has determined that men cannot be motivated, under its principles, to act for the good of society. Men would only appear to do so when their individual interests coincided with the general happiness. But when a conflict occurred between their interest and that of society, the latter would be disregarded. As Jouffroy says: "The principle of general utility is a lie; the rule which effectively operates is personal utility."

Bentham bases his legal system on the principle of utility because he does not recognize the Supreme Being, author of divine law which governs the moral universe. For example, in discussing crimes not covered by the law, he says:

To explain why human laws fail to cover all crimes against mankind, some men have found it useful to indoctrinate others with the belief in a Supreme Invisible Being, a power above the law, to whom is attributed

---

6 The French philosopher, Théodore Simon Jouffroy (1796–1842).

the will of maintaining the laws of society and the power of punishing and rewarding the actions of men where the law has been remiss or too limited. The Supreme Being, God, has been invented because some men believed it would be useful as a means of checking crimes that exceed the power of human law to punish. Although he makes a note at this point to obviate his being called an atheist, that accusation would still be correct. If he believed in a Supreme Being he would not say that it was believed useful to indoctrinate men with this belief, nor would he say that this power has been attributed by men to what they have invented. In the same note, he says that it is impossible for men to offend God; to say this is a heresy that history refutes. There are countless examples of God's punishment of men for their sins. His comment also contradicts the dogma of the redemption of sin.

*   *   *

Mons. Guizot,[7] the French Protestant and moralist whose wisdom and integrity are unquestioned, has said this in opposition to Bentham's doctrine:

I have proved that moral law is not convention nor a human creation; still less is it one of the necessary laws that rule the material world. It is the law of the intellectual, free world. It is a law which is superior to those of this world. Whoever recognizes this achieves at once freedom and servitude. Who is the author of this law? Who imposes it on man and who governs him without enslaving him? Who has put it in the world where man spends his present life? Evidently there is a supreme power from whom this moral law emanates as a manifestation of himself. With the good sense that frequently caused Voltaire to forget his frivolity and cynicism, he said of the material world and the order operating in it: "I cannot believe this watch exists unless there is a watchmaker."

In the moral order, we deal with something more important than a watch: we find ourselves in the presence of a machine that has been regulated once and for all time. The law

of order, that is to say the moral law, is always in conflict with human liberty. Liberty pays homage to law; it can obey it or violate it. Law manifests the Supreme Legislator of whom it is thought and will. God, moral sovereign, and man, free subject, are alike contained in moral law. Kant found God in moral law; unfortunately, he could not find Him elsewhere. One thing is certain, however, that it is in moral law, the governor of human liberty, where God most vividly reveals himself to man.

For the same reason, a moral law without a legislator who imposes it on man would be an inexplicable fact; it would be like a river without a source. Inexplicable also would be the fact of free man's moral responsibility without a Supreme Judge to whom he is responsible; this would be like a river flowing meaninglessly in all directions instead of following its course to the sea. And just as the moral law reveals a moral legislator, so does moral responsibility reveal a judge of morals. Just as the moral law is not a law of human authorship so are human judgments, purported to be morally responsible, rarely the perfect judgment that this responsibility demands. God is in moral law as its original author and in moral responsibility as its definitive judge. The moral order, which is the entirety of moral law, is incomprehensible and impossible without God's establishing it in relation to the liberty of man. God will reestablish it when the liberty of man transforms it.

Thus the moral facts inherent and proper to human nature are: the reality of good and evil; and man's moral obligation, moral liberty, and moral responsibility. All are intimately connected with the facts of religion, which are: God, the moral legislator; God, spectator and moral judge. Morality is naturally and essentially linked with religion.

All that Guizot has said is clear, natural, and logical. By this unique sanction alone can the social order be maintained. Here is the moralist raising his face to Heaven; Bentham beats his against the earth. Bentham mocks all this by saying that there are arbitrary principles of sympathy and antipathy. He says that one man wants to impose his opinions on others. To do this, he has recourse to whatever he can invent, and disguises the despotism of his thought by ingenious phrases. Bentham adds:

[7] Francois Pierre Guillaume Guizot (1787–1874).

Almost all the systems of moral philosophy prove this. A man tells us that there is a certain thing in him — called conscience — that has been given to him to teach him what is good and evil. The most ingenious of these despots frankly states: "I am one of the chosen. God has instructed his chosen ones what is good and what is evil."

In Bentham's view, the arbitrary principle of antipathy and sympathy accounts for the origin of moral systems founded on a belief in God. "The worst enemies of the principle of utility," he says,

are those systems founded on what is called the religious principle. Their advocates profess to take the will of God as the only test of good or evil. I say to them that this religious principle is the same as several others we have examined. It illustrates the principle of antipathy and sympathy.

The moral philosophy of Mons. Guizot which we have just examined, then, is not based on reason but on antipathy and sympathy, for Bentham believes materialism contains all reason.

In *Ethics*, Bentham refutes the dogma of hell and eternal punishment. "This terrible dogma," he says, "is not part of Christianity. It has been perniciously added. You will not find it anywhere in the Holy Scripture."

It is difficult to believe that a man of average intelligence could say such a thing. Of course, when this sophist supports his remarks by the authority of Holy Scripture, he does not do so because he believes in the Bible. Rather he intends to surprise his readers, who believe in the Bible but do not know it well, by making a daring assertion. What other reason would there be for an author of legislation to speak in this manner without having read the Holy Scripture? Doubtless in his calculations he would lose less if he were caught in a lie than he would profit if he won converts away from the belief he says is "useful to indoctrinate man with." But what has the Holy Scripture to say on the dogma of eternal punishments?

Speaking to his disciples about the final judgment to be passed on the quick and the dead, Jesus Christ mentioned first the glorious sentence of the good. Then he said: "Begone from me, accursed ones, to the eternal fire that has been prepared for the devil and his angels!" What is most astonishing is that Bentham would make it a crime to diminish belief in eternal punishment because such belief serves the State. In combatting the belief, Bentham himself commits the crime. What a legislator!

Among the crimes against religion he cites pernicious dogmas that include those of Catholicism.

Catholicism persecutes learned men, makes brutes of people, fills men with terror, and prohibits them from enjoying innocent pleasures; it is the most dangerous enemy of morals and law.

He says that this enemy should be attacked by free inquiry, that is, by Protestantism. Now we know why Benthamists, who believe in no religion, support Protestantism.

The character of this work does not permit us to enter into a formal examination of the errors of the Benthamist system but we cannot overlook his immoral, antisocial doctrines. Under "Crimes against the People," he lists suicide, emigration, abortion, voluntary celibacy, and fornication.

I make this list only to point out the common error of regarding these acts as detrimental to the population; actually, they do not have any perceptible influence on it.

Could there be worse doctrines for society? Worse ones to teach young men in the *colegios*? It is well known that prostitutes are sterile, and, if fornication is a matter of indifference, the majority of the female population who have no idea of honor will dedicate themselves to this free industry. Since a great part of the population, then, will not procreate, and the number of marriages will decline because men find ready means to satisfy their carnal passion, the population will decline. All statesmen except Bentham recognize that an increase in marriages is the primary means of increasing population. This is a population, moreover, that is useful to society for it has the nurture of a regular family.

Bentham says that there are no crimes against oneself, properly speaking, but only errors of calculation because one wants to experience pleasure, not pain. This would justify all hidden sins, solitary pleasures, and lewd thoughts and acts. What a frightening thought! According to the moral sensualist, any act is licit that causes no alarm to society. Bentham and his commentator therefore justify suicide, infanticide, abortion, and any corruption of customs necessary to conceal crimes; neither priest nor parents would be able to prevent the total corruption of family life which would surely ensue.

As we have seen, Bentham tried to support his denial of the dogma of eternal punishments on the Holy Scripture. Now he justifies the most atrocious of crimes by the example of Jesus Christ, As he says in *Ethics*:

One cannot say that Jesus Christ has prohibited suicide. His own example shows that it is justified in some cases, for he was master of his own destiny and submitted voluntarily to death.

Jesus Christ was God, author of nature, master of life and death. He could put his life down and take it up again. He told the Jews:

I lay down my life to take it up again. No one takes it from me, I lay it down of my own accord. I have power to lay it down and power to take it up again.

Man, the creature, has he power to lay his life down and take it up again? Can a man who commits suicide revive himself as Jesus Christ did? If man could take up his life again after laying it down, suicide would not be a crime; it would be like lying down to sleep and awakening. How then

can the sophist attribute to the creature the power and acts of the Creator? Is it because Bentham does not believe that Jesus Christ was God? The commentator Salas supports this idea by saying that since man is the master of himself he can dispose of himself as he will. Listen, then, to the general rule that Bentham gives to legislators for judging crimes against self:

Leave the greatest possible latitude to individuals in all cases where they harm no one but themselves because they are the best judges of their own interests.

The reader can judge by these explanations that we have made of Bentham's principles whether this legislation can be taught to youth without any risk of perverting their religious beliefs and customs. We believe that even if Doctor Margalló were the professor at the Colegio of San Bartolomé, and he argued against the doctrines of Bentham, the students would still choose sensualism, because they were prepared for it by the philosophy of Tracy.

In spite of the torrent of public protest, the doctrines of Bentham continued to be taught. And if the theory of this author about the evil resulting from a general alarm is true, then both that evil and another have come to Colombia. But the evil resulting from the general state of alarm caused by the teaching of sensualist materialism would never be as great as the evil which originated with the government.

Did the government believe in Bentham's principles? Did it support them because it was persuaded of their truth? Then why did it not suppress such teaching on seeing the great alarm that it caused in society? Isn't whatever causes alarm in society a crime? Then the government committed a crime in supporting the teaching of Bentham and placed itself in contradiction with Bentham himself. Let us say, then, that the government of Colombia and its chosen ones had other reasons, of wider significance, for supporting this program of education.

The Fatal Contamination of Secularism

MARIANO CUEVAS, S.J.

Born in Mexico City, Mariano Cuevas (1879–   ) entered the order of the Society of Jesus in 1893 and was ordained in 1909. A professor of history in various Jesuit colleges including those at Saltillo and Puebla, Father Cuevas has been for Mexico what Groot was for Colombia, a champion of Catholicism. Like Groot, he has witnessed civil wars in which free thought as opposed to unity of faith was a paramount issue. The editor of many works and bodies of documents dealing with colonial Mexico, Father Cuevas has preferred to encompass the broad sweep of Mexican history in his writings, as suggested by *History of the Church in Mexico*, 5 vols. (1921–28), and *History of the Mexican Nation*, 3 vols. (1940). That Father Cuevas represents a continuing, if currently subordinated, part of Mexican civilization is suggested in the appearance of the fifth edition of his work on the Church in 1946–47, and in a second edition of his general history in 1952–3. The following selection is from his history of the Church.

FROM what was explained in the first two parts of this volume, our readers have been made familiar with the last years of the only period of *life* that New Spain has enjoyed — the two centuries from 1572 to 1765. During this time, our country spent its youth in the shadow of the Church; these formative years were sane and serene, years that might have been the herald of an exceptional prosperity rising from no other influence than the shaping forces of the past.

But unfortunately the union with Spain that until 1765 had resulted in a balance of good and evil, was of advantage to Mexico, and redounded to the glory of the mother country, became the source of our moral ruin.

I do not deny that some Mexicans — especially certain social classes — were partly to blame for this condition, nor do I deny that a large part of our clergy was apathetic or negligent. Let it be granted also that these moral calamities we are going to describe are to be attributed more to the climate of the times than to Spain herself. If the reader will judge by what I am about to present, however, I think he will concede that had it been possible to generate a well-planned, bloodless, and sane independence movement, Mexico, like a good daughter who has reached a marriageable age, would have, as a result, left the house of her parents with their blessing and advice, and our nation would have traveled a different road from the painful one on which she has sought redemption since 1765.

The evil inflicted on us from approximately 1765 did not begin, like a germ that causes tuberculosis, its slow destruction from the inside, but struck like an epidemic that lays a healthy young man in his grave in a few days. During two centuries, death could not come to us from the healthful moral and religious climate of the West; it came from the change in that Western climate which destroyed people everywhere.

From Mariano Cuevas, *Historia de la Iglesia en Mexico*, 5 vols. (5th ed.: Mexico, 1946–47), IV, pp. 435–451, 538–540. Used by permission of Editorial Patria, S.A.

The French-style army established among us in the fatal year of 1765 was the first, if not necessarily the greatest, of the evils inflicted on us. Formerly, about 3,000 soldiers, most of whom were our own countrymen, protected the immense Viceroyalty of New Spain including Texas, California, and the islands. But the threat of attack by England, the military bent of Viceroy Marquis of Cruillas,[1] and especially the conviction of the Madrid government that only by a large army could unpopular measures already planned be enforced — all these considerations lay behind the sending of this army to what was until then a peaceful, contented New Spain.

On Nov. 1, 1765, Lieutenant General Don Juan de Villalba, disembarked in Veracruz; he had been sent to organize the army. He was accompanied by five field marshals, many officers of lower rank, and 2,000 Swiss and Walloon soldiers.

The inhabitants now began to leave the hearth for the barracks. They no longer regarded themselves as ordinary people for they were now members of a privileged and superior class on whom peace, law enforcement, and administration depended. After being armed and trained, the army became conscious not only of its power but of the fact that its power was made secure by the arms it possessed. The destiny of the colony and the later Mexican Republic were now at the mercy of the army; all future efforts of the people to throw off the yoke of the army would be fruitless.

From these comments, which are made by a liberal general, not a priest, the reader will discern the two evils he points out: immorality guaranteed by military *compañerismo* [presumably the vices associated with barracks life] and the perversion of justice under the ordinary law.

Besides these evils, the foreign army brought with it others that were much greater. This deluge of impious foreigners, Lutherans, Calvinists, or simply scoundrels and blasphemers from Naples and Sicily,

were the dregs of Europe, recruited as mercenaries by Charles III. As cadres, they became the model for the rank and file of mulatos and the poorer *mestizos* in places like Veracruz; these poor people suddenly found themselves in the militia, surrounded by gold braid and epaulettes. Moreover, they were envied by their humble fellow men who did not have the honor of rubbing elbows with these new masters, lords wearing three-cornered hats and jackets *a la francesa.*

The officers brought something worse than the soldiers did: the first germs of Masonry [Freemasonry], which already had contaminated Spain. The army in New Spain became a source of continual disturbance of the public peace; crimes involving the use of arms occurred with increasing frequency and the wrongdoers escaped punishment because of military protection. The boldness of militiamen increased the more they felt themselves beyond the reach of the law.

But the greatest evidence of the evil influence of the army was manifested in the torrent of accusations of impiety and blasphemy that poured into the offices of the Holy Inquisition. Cases involving soldiers and especially those of the Regiment of America multiplied. Antonio Chacolete, an Italian, was brought before the Inquisition for irreverent use of a picture of San Antonio[2] that a painter had sold him at his barracks. José Indán, Nicolás Servín, a Genoese; Sagismundo Wolfres, José María Rezzonico, Pedro Fulcheri, Sebastián San Jorge, Juan Jaime Moret, Pedro Fiolí, and even the drummer José María Abat — all soldiers of the Regiment of America, were tried for committing impious and scandalous acts that could have been conceived only by irreligious minds. Nor was the Regiment of Dragoons free from such contamination; Juan Urritialde, José Minguillón, José Francisco Dueñas, Diego de Oroz, Manuel de Ocejo, and others were tried for blasphemy or heretical acts. Similar impi-

[1] Joaquín Monserrat, Marquis of Cruillas, who was viceroy from 1760 to 1766.

[2] St. Anthony (c. 250–350), first Christian monk.

eties occurred in other parts of the army including the battalions of Ultonia, Flanders, and Migueletes. The militia was infected by the same disease as a result of contact with foreign soldiers.

*   *   *

The evil caused by these soldiers in time of war was exceeded only by the evil they caused in peacetime, for then their relatives and friends who flocked to Mexico had a truly pernicious influence on the country. Spanish immigrants of the lowest type made common cause with them. The immigrants from Spain were the conquistadors until the middle of the 16th century; until the end of the following century, the immigrants were highwaymen and rogues. Then during the early part of the eighteenth century, immigrants arrived who were beneficial to the country. Coming from northern Spain, they were more industrious and stauncher in the faith than any other inhabitants of the country. As a rule, these men settled permanently in Mexico; many of our most respected families now bear their names.

But the army brought a mob of corrupted people, corrupted not alone in customs but in ideas. Listen to the significant description that four prelates of New Spain wrote to the king on October 24, 1761:

There used to come to the Indies from Spain immigrants with official positions who had been sent because they were so quarrelsome they could not be tolerated in Spain, or because no position could be found for them there. They came only to get rich and return. If there was an illegitimate son in a Spanish family, he is invariably sent to the Indies. If a young man who has promised to marry a girl, or has got her with child, wishes to escape his obligation he flees to the Indies. He boards some ship as a stowaway, or pretends to be a boatswain, or the servant of an official or another passenger.

This occurs regularly in spite of prohibitions against it. Spain, as a result, is being slowly depopulated and this kingdom is filled with men motivated only by avarice or a desire to live without God, king, or law.

Mexico could at present be called a universal colony because foreign regiments, contraband vessels, and those pretending to be Spaniards, come here from other nations. Although royal orders prohibiting this have been received in New Spain, they are not enforced; worse, an Englishman pretending to be a Spaniard, or some other astute heretic, can pervert this kingdom, corrupt its religion and customs, and plant bad seeds that will cause a decline in loyalty to the legitimate sovereign and in respect for what is sacred. These foreigners will cause dogma to be treated with contempt and will contribute to a regrettable and infernal libertinage that will destroy the piety instilled into the Indians by long missionary labor and the devoutness of the Spaniards. Bishops and priests will despair and utter confusion will reign.

We appeal to Your Majesty, confident that he is our father, our asylum, and our protector. We know that rarely does anyone speak frankly to Your Majesty about the state of these provinces; for us, it would be a sin to keep silence. It is necessary, our lord and king, to prohibit any foreigner from entering these provinces, which are coveted more than any others by foreign powers; they direct their main efforts at trying to capture these provinces during time of war. Let the law apply only to the future for it might have serious consequences to try to uproot the evils committed in the past.

We shall comment here how painful it is to see that the bishops believed their only remedy was to appeal to their father, their asylum, and their protector. They were putting their trust in Charles III, so evil and so inept as to be the cause himself of these evils. This was the precise moment when the bishops, recognizing that they alone were the real moral force in New Spain, should have taken the only possible remedy; the road of a noble independence. But it is very rare to find men with the temperament and point of view to take these steps.

The bishops continue their letter:

Let those who come to these kingdoms for government positions (high or low, bishoprics or governorships) be chosen not from those who solicit them with gifts, but from those who refuse to resort to bribery; not from those who are meddlesome, but from those who are moderate and just; not from those who aspire to acquiring a *mayorazgo* [entailed estate] or a palace at the cost of the blood of these poor Indians, but from those who perform their duties disinterestedly and are honest in their handling of public funds; let greedy and knavish officials and bad administrators be called to Spain without serving their full terms.

We are not saying that there have not always been scandals and evil in the world. We only want to prevent the greatest evil so that this kingdom might be the best governed of the Americas, might serve Your Majesty better than it has served him, might contain the most contented vassals, and might nourish the most flourishing Catholic faith (the bishops should have said, the *only* faith). We only want God to protect these kingdoms from envious foreign powers for the sake of the royal, august, pious(!), amiable, just(!), ever Catholic family of Your Majesty. Those powers, although also Christian, have depreciated the motives of the conquest, and denigrated its high purposes. They have tried to weaken your military power. In their histories, they have stained the character of Spaniards and Indians and they have prophesied the decadence or the disloyalty of your dominions. In their colonies, the main idol is Mercury, god of the merchants; Venus, who attracts the colonists, and Mars, whom they believe is the source of all law and power. These foreigners abhor bishops, with their robes and the crosses that they wear on their chests; they abominate chastity, and despise religion, which they artfully depict as useless to the state. They hope to deceive the world so that all people will become atheists and Machiavellians. In their view, religion would continue formally but in essence would be a slave to the constitution of the state. Bishops would become mere mouthpieces of the state, saying only what the state permits. Men, endowed with reason and immortal souls, would become beasts for whom death is the determinate end. Materialists make men into donkeys without more purpose in life than to eat and drink.

So much for the account of the bishops. Although they were mistaken in their remedies, their diagnosis and profound description of the country was prescient. Of course,

they were voices crying in the desert, for the reforms they asked for were not carried out.

The Inquisition continued to try, if not to punish, pernicious foreigners. Some of the cases, which we have copied from documents for the years 1763 and 1765 were: . . . The Englishman, William Jalafan, a carpenter living in Veracruz, who said whenever religion was discussed in his presence: "Let's drop that subject and just try to eat, drink, and live." Dr. José Mariano Gordón, who referred to the Pope and his indulgences as a plague, and when Don Carlos de Lorenzana, one of the outstanding members of the community brought up a religious subject, Gordón said to him: "You believe in your law and I'll believe in mine, and on Judgment Day we'll see whose conduct was right." Another of these contaminated persons was Fr. Pedro Rodríguez, a native of Andalusia, who spoke several languages, had lived in Martinique, and was a recluse in a Franciscan convent and apparently a spy for the English. Diego Mackenzie and his companions, Juan Enrique Stron, Tomás Sewiun, and Carlos Artonk, all Protestants living as reconciled Catholics in Veracruz.

But the French were the most numerous of the foreigners. Antonio Guilliar, who had been a cook for many years, was imprisoned in a secret jail as a Lutheran and Calvinist. He had been earlier baptized as a Gentile and put in a convent, but he escaped and was not apprehended for some time. Nicolas Masy, who lived in Mexico City with a Genoese midwife as his mistress, mocked at religious processions and ridiculed priests; he was secretly imprisoned in the viceregal palace but was later freed. The surgeons Don Francisco Desplán and Don Reinaldo Thomás, residents of Mexico City, who said that the custom of saying the Ave Maria daily was nonsense and landscapes of the country should be hung in public salons instead of the pictures of saints. José Gelede, also a surgeon, who lived in Tabasco, called the Spanish idolatrous and laughed when he visited a sick person and found candles burning for the saints. Marcos Antonio Cluer de la Milliere, living in Mexico City, who asked sick persons what limbo was; Antonio Olier, in Sonsonate, who was accused of making similar statements of derogatory intent concerning the Eucharist and the power of God. Especially should the case of Daniel Marcotun be mentioned. An Irishman, an ensign of the Regiment of Orduña, he was denounced as a Freemason in May, 1770; his case was the subject of a long investigation by the Council of the Indies.

The inquisitors were very far from being apathetic. They made serious efforts to deal with heresies as is indicated by two letters, one of April 28, and another of August 24, 1766, to the Supreme Tribunal. Such dates indicate their prompt attention to the first symptoms of contamination from the newly arrived army. In the first letter, they wrote:

Denunciations of many of the foreign soldiers who came with the troops from Spain have been increasing daily. Although most of the cases have not been important enough to warrant action by the Holy Office, we are convinced that the soldiers denounced are motivated by a hatred for the faith that they do not dare to reveal openly. They speak only in innuendos for fear of punishment and offending the local inhabitants that they have begun to associate with. What may be gleaned from their explanations is that they are sympathetic to Lutheranism and Calvinism or, what is worse, that some recognize no religion or sect. What is most harmful about this is that their impious comments are usually accompanied by praise for the English nation, so that the likely effect on the inhabitants is on the one hand, to weaken their faith and on the other, to lessen their hatred of the English, whom they have despised as heretics. We already face the threat to our future of a decline in faith that has made the inhabitants receptive to opinions contrary to its purity; the comments favorable to the English government also persuade those people, if not to like that government, at least to abandon the ancient hatred for it which they have so long held.

This fear would not be illusory if during an invasion by the enemy, when a defense of the kingdom was sorely needed, these people turned out to be our enemy — not the enemy of the English. Perhaps they might declare themselves not only partisans of the enemy but might try to win others to their side, taking advantage of the fears aroused by the invasion.

Thus ends the comments of the Inquisitors. This last paragraph makes it clear that some of our countrymen have been bought by Protestantism.

There is no doubt, then, that the Mexican Inquisition retained its sense of duty and its desire to heal the many mortal wounds which our faithful and pious country had received in a few years. But in Spain matters were much worse for there the Inquisition had declined because of the influence of leading statesmen who surrounded the throne. Doubtless the Mexican officials received orders to relax the investigation, prosecution, and especially the punishment of crimes against the faith. D. Vicente de la Fuente [(1817–1889), Spanish church historian] describes the position of the Holy Inquisition in Spain this way:

It was said that during the reign of Charles III there already was a desire to suppress the Tribunal of the Inquisition. Roda presented to the king several documents to prove that the question of its suppression had already been considered during the reigns of Philip the Handsome, Charles V, and Philip V, or in other words, when foreign kings assumed the throne. Charles III's answer to Roda[3] was simply: "The Spanish want it, and it doesn't disturb me." To curb the power of the Inquisition, some partial measures were then carried out. These included prohibiting the inquisitors from banning the work of any living writer without giving him a hearing where he could explain what significance he intended in it. Sometime later the Inquisition charged the ministers Roda, Campomanes, Aranda, and Floridablanca,[4] and the bishops who comprised the Extraordinary Council of 1767, with philosophism [following French thought]

---

[3] Manuel Roda y Arrieta, Marquis of Roda, Spanish statesman.

[4] Pedro Rodríguez, Count of Campomanes (1723–1802), Pedro Pablo Abarca de Bolea, Count of Aranda(1719–1798), José Moñino y Redondo, Count of Florida Blanca (1728–1808).

and Jansenism.[5] Its accusation furnished an excuse to reduce its power still further by placing ministers who defended the regalia of the crown outside inquisitorial jurisdiction. A royal *cedula* of 1770 prescribed that the Inquisition would in the future have cognizance only in cases of obstinate heresy and apostasy; cases of blasphemy, bigamy, sodomy and others formerly of its cognizance, would be heard by ordinary tribunals. Still later (1784) sentences passed by the Inquisition on any titled person, minister of the king, officer of the army, or magistrate, were subject to review by the king.

To sum up, by the end of the last century and the beginning of the present one [nineteenth century], the Inquisition was only a shadow of its former self. It decayed still more because of the liking of the Inquisitor Arce for Godoy[6] and because of French influence on the latter.

*   *   *

Books containing impious and heretical ideas, which were imported from Europe, caused us more harm than impious persons did. The praiseworthy efforts of the Catholic Kings of the House of Austria to prevent this intellectual poison from getting into the hands of their people is well known. They did what any father would who loves his children. We have only to read Title 24 of Book 1 of the *Recopilación de Indias* [colonial law code] to be convinced of the truth of this statement. The Inquisition had besides the law, an abundance of instructions, which they used to prevent the export of books from Spain harmful to our faith and customs. The Inquisitors of Mexico certainly performed these duties well when they were given full power to protect the faith.

Until the middle of the eighteenth century, the Inquisitors censored books that were of only moderate danger to the faith;

after that time, however, the books that they tried to ban were positively impious French works, either in Spanish translation or in the original language.

The good Mexican Inquisitors, supposing they had the same support in Madrid as formerly, wrote in alarm (and as it turned out naively) to the crown on May 26, 1769:

The libertinage in thought which has begun to spread in these kingdoms, originated with European soldiers and other foreigners in this capital. There is no ready cure for this incipient plague. We are finding it daily more difficult to carry out our duties. Any work speaking against royal authority is read and freely discussed. Respect for bishops is deteriorating and the priestly character is an object of scorn. The most venerable objects of our faith are being taken from their sanctuaries and exposed to the eyes of the profane. These objects are not now considered mysteries for the impious have their own explanations for them. Their arrogance has reached the point that they are not content with knowing what it is fitting to know; they now attack even the idea of religion. In this condition of liberty, the books of Voltaire and of L'Metrie,[7] among other wicked books, enter the country as Your Majesty will see by the testimony in cases of this nature. The army, vitiated in its customs, is infected with impious attitudes and heretical ideas.

The multitude of foreigners who for various reasons have come to this kingdom threatens its ruin if corrective action is not soon taken. But we do not have enough ministers to discharge the obligations of our office.

In this situation which was so dangerous for the faith, the Inquisitors brought to the attention of the Spanish ministry an issue of the *Gaceta de Madrid* in which the famous bull, *In coena Domini* was discussed. On the advice of the bishop of Puebla, they confiscated several copies of the work of Justino Febronio,[8] in the customs office

---

[5] A reformed Catholicism advocated by the French theologian Cornelius Jansen (1585–1638).

[6] Juan de Arce y Otalora; Manuel Godoy, Duke of Alcudia (1767–1851), who was the power behind the throne at this time.

[7] Presumably the French physician and philosopher Julien Offray de Lamettrie (1709–1751).

[8] "Justinus Febronius," pseudonym of Johann Nikolaus von Hontheim (1701–1790), German

and even took custody of some handkerchiefs which bore the inscription: *vox populi vox Dei*.[9] But they were later obliged by the ministry to let the *gacetas* circulate and to return to their owners the copies of the work they had confiscated. This means that the Madrid ministry had cut the wings of the Inquisition and, preparatory to issuing a decree abolishing it, was gradually restricting its power. On the other hand, the ministry had the inquisitors, bishops, and viceroys of America searching for the books and papers written in defense of the banished Company of Jesus. They considered the writing of these works a crime of *lese-majesté* and prohibited anyone from reading them under penalty of death.

As if all these evils were not enough, members of the Holy Tribunal were unfaithful to their offices either because of discouragement or because they too were corrupted. On one occasion it was discovered that an employee of the Holy Office had sold to someone in Mexico City — for 850 pesos — the prohibited books the Inquisition had earlier confiscated.

The source of the main elements of the destruction of our faith — not hidden to be sure — was in the Spanish Crown itself. This source was not confined to the monarchs themselves, but included the *camarillas* of ministers that surrounded them.

Since Spain became Bourbonized, the germs of great evil contaminated that most Christian nation; even today it has not been disinfected. As soon as the cause of Philip V triumphed (say rather the cause of Louis XIV) over that of the pretenders of the House of Austria, good Catholics who had supported the Bourbons saw that not only did the crown pass to a French monarch, but positions at the court did also. A French *camarilla* soon pushed out the great Spanish figures including Cardinal Portocarrero; the genuinely Spanish spirit of that court was also driven out. Many years would pass before a very noble and very Spanish Bourbon king[10] would once more place Spain on the high and independent throne which rests where Isabel the Catholic had placed it — on the live rock of our Holy Faith.

The French *camarilla*, which was installed by Louis XIV as soon as his relative ascended the throne, now kicked out the ladder by which it had ascended. Portocarrero, the archbishop of Seville, and Don Manuel Arias, president of the Council, realized that the age of Cisneros[11] was over. They were replaced by the French cardinal D'Estrees, who played the role of Mazzarino [a cardinal at Paris] discussing questions of court etiquette with the Princess of Ursinos.[12] The archbishops of Toledo and Seville fled from such a court. Louis XIV sent the French financial expert Orry [Jean Orry (1652–1719)] to Madrid to reorganize the royal treasury; Orry at once eyed the property of the church.

Also during this time, the principle of regalism, which had always existed to some extent in Spain as it had in other European countries, was much strengthened and expanded by new laws. To profess regalism was of great aid to anyone aspiring to a position in the court and even in the Church. That tendency of regalism to absorb the rights and liberties of the Church, apparent even under the Habsburgs, became truly alarming under Philip V. But it would be true to say that Macanaz[13] and his contemporaries were not as impious or scornful toward the Holy See as Spanish ministers were fifty years later. They were very far from being as irreligious as those in power at the end of this accursed eighteenth century.

But regalism and the corruption of customs at the court were preparing the ground for the reception of heresies. Contributing

theologian who advocated a national Catholicism later called Febronianism.

[9] The voice of the people is the voice of God.

[10] Possibly a reference to Alphonso XIII, who was exiled in 1931.

[11] Francisco Jiménez de Cisneros (1436–1517), clergyman, and one of the great Spanish statesmen.

[12] Marie Anne de la Tremoille, Princesse des Ursins (1642–1722), the main power behind the throne from 1701–14.

[13] Melchor Rafael de Macanaz (1670–1760), Spanish statesman and diplomat.

to this preparation also was the substitution of weak, easygoing confessors of the king for energetic, keen-minded ones. Thus prepared, the court and the army were infected by Masonry imported from England. The first Masonic lodge was established in Madrid in 1728 in a hotel on San Bernardo Street. Masonry spread so rapidly that in 1739 a provincial Grand Master was named for Andalusia.

Philip V, aware that the source of Masonry was in England, and urged to move against it by a bull of Pope Clement XII, had several members of the Madrid lodge imprisoned. Nonetheless the lodges continued to multiply; in 1750 the Supreme Tribunal of the Inquisition had a list naming ninety-seven of them.

With the death penalty against Masons decreed by the good king Ferdinand VI in 1751, and with the bull of Pope Benedict XIV, which opened the eyes of those unaware of the dangers of Masonic principles, Spanish Masonry, or Anglo-Spanish Masonry rather, was nearly eliminated.

Soon, however, Charles III arrived at the court from Naples; with him came a swarm of Volterians among whom Masonry would find hospitality. By 1767 there were many lodges and Masonry was so influential that a grand Spanish lodge was established with Don Pedro Abarca de Bolea, Count of Aranda, as the first Grand Master. Prominent members included Don Pedro Rodríguez Campomanes, D. Miguel Manuel de Nava, Don Pedro del Río and Don Luis Valle Salazar. In this faction of renegades and their protégés, all motivated by a hatred for religion and by an un-Spanish attitude inspired by England, is the source of all our evil.

*   *   *

We have already said that the Inquisition could not now be counted on. Although it was not legally abolished, its existence was merely formal in Mexico; in Spain it was a ridiculous comedy because the members of the Inquisition were its own enemies.

The Mexican Inquisition not only was weakened and relaxed its persecution of impiety because of orders received from Spain, but during the last decade of the century it perverted its own purposes. It concentrated mainly on the ever-increasing number of persons suspected of working for independence; by this action the Inquisition became not only useless to the church but actually antagonistic toward it. The inscription above its door that reads: "For the terror of heresy, security of these kingdoms, and the honor of God," should have been changed to: "For espionage and the persecution of the Mexicans."

Although points of religion were considered in the loose, apathetic manner of the age, the main purpose of the judges was to emphasize crimes against the state in inquisitorial cases. Consider the case of Pablo Juan Catadiano, a thirty-four-year-old Basque, who was a commission merchant in Mexico City. He was denounced on September 3, 1794, for making statements against religion and the State. He was said to approve of the execution of the King of France and of French political principles that were considered subversive. After hearing his case, the Inquisitorial Court sentenced him to be severely reprimanded by the court, to be exiled forever from America, and to disavow his statements in the presence of twelve merchants in the courtroom of the Inquisition. At Veracruz, in February, 1796, he was put on a ship for Cádiz.

Among the cases involving religion and the state was that of the Frenchman Juan Laurel, chief cook of the Count of Revillagigedo.[14] He was imprisoned in Jalapa. The inquisitors wrote to the Crown:

We have passed this sentence because of a statement given us by the viceroy, Marquis of Branciforte,[15] and because of the case that we drew up as a result against this enemy of the faith and the state. Inspired by the French

[14] Juan Vicente de Güemes y Pacheco de Padilla, second Conde de Revillagigedo, who was viceroy from 1789–94.

[15] Miguel de la Grúa y Branciforte, Marquis of Branciforte, who was viceroy from July 12, 1794–May 31, 1798.

Revolution and the present form of government of France, French residents in this kingdom and Frenchified Spaniards are attempting to spread their abominable doctrine of liberty and impiety.

Here are some details that the Inquisitor General mentioned in a private letter concerned with the revolutionary movement of ideas in Mexico City. The perverse French who sow discord and disloyalty everywhere cannot ignore this country, the source of much silver. Those resident here, especially the artisans, wigmakers, and watchmakers, have grown insolent and capable of causing untold harm because we have complacently ignored their influence among us.

On the night of August 26, 1794, a seditious pasquinade, which was derogatory toward our Catholic faith and monarchical government and approved of the French government, appeared in a public place. The new viceroy, zealous in the service of God and king, commissioned the *alcalde* for criminal cases, Don Pedro Valenzuela, to take charge of the case; this in turn encouraged us to take action for the *alcalde* has great confidence in the Inquisition and in each of the Inquisitors.

Although the author of the pasquinade was not found in spite of a thorough investigation, plans for a kingdom-wide rebellion were discovered. The rebellion was to begin with an armed uprising in the capital, which aimed to eliminate the leaders of secular and ecclesiastical government, and the Inquisitors.

So far the main conspirators seem to have been a French surgeon and an Andalusian noble, but doubtless there are many accomplices including Frenchmen, creoles, and *gachupines* or European Spaniards. Since the seeds of rebellion were widely sown, there have been many prisoners. This tribunal, without exceeding its laws, has apprehended some persons. We have received many denunciations and shall spare nothing in pursuing these wild beasts disguised as men with whom we are struggling.

But the seed planted by the French soon sprouted and grew. . . .

From what has been described it could be said that the Mexican Church ended the eighteenth century and began the following one with both arms broken — the arm of the Inquisition and that of the Church-led schools. The head of the Church, the episcopacy, was confused; the body of the nation, the aristocracy, was infected by Masonry, and afflicted with the cancer of impiety.

The Spanish Liberals and the Clergy

JUAN MANUEL HERRERO

After his graduation from the University of Valladolid, Juan Manuel Herrero was appointed professor of Universal and Modern History at the University of Seville. His most recent appointment was to the Chair of Geography and History at the *Instituto de Enseñanza Media* at Melilla. Like several other post-civil-war Spanish historians, Dr. Herrero writes well-documented history that reflects both wide reading and careful analysis. In the selection that follows, Dr. Herrero praises the Spanish liberals for their patriotism and optimism but concludes, nonetheless, that the principles of liberal utilitarianism and traditional religion could not, and cannot, be reconciled. Spaniards had to decide which view of life would claim their loyalty.

By THE second half of the eighteenth century, important changes had taken place in Spain. A new social class, the bourgeoisie, had risen to such importance that their representative figures aspired to political power in order to defend bourgeois rights and to acquire privileges denied them under the old order based on the three estates. New forms of wealth and new currents of thought also threatened the base of the Old Regime which was too small to make room for these new elements. Logically, the bourgeoisie have been in opposition to the traditional order and its ideology; bourgeois economists and political essayists offered new solutions for old problems. I have elsewhere given examples of these writings from letters chosen from the *Spanish Epistolario of the Eighteenth Century,* found in the Rivadeneyra collection.

In the *Epistolario,* the letters of Cabarrús[1] are outstanding because of their large number and importance; Cabarrús well represents one of the tendencies that can be observed in the bourgeois ideology of the

time. During these years, a divergence of opinion arose among bourgeois thinkers, especially regarding the position taken on such fundamental matters as reason and tradition, forms of government, and the position of the church in society.

In analyzing a later period (1814) [Federico] Suárez Verdeguer identified three positions: those supporting the Old Regime, the "liberal-reformist group" and the "royalist-reformist group." The precedents for the last two groups are found in the eighteenth century for bourgeois ideology is as much rooted in Carlist[2] thought as in liberal thought.

Although the ideas connected with these political divisions are not well studied, I have in mind these last two groups when I classify many of the statements contained in the *Epistolario* as preliberal. At the same time, there was another tendency in bourgeois thought that we can call, under the

[1] Francisco Cabarrús, Count of Cabarrús (1752–1810), a naturalized Spaniard born in Bayonne.

[2] In 19th-century Spain, Spaniards who wished to return to the traditional Spanish liberties of the patrimonial state and to a protected unity of faith, supported various pretenders to the throne named Charles. Hence their ideas have been called Carlism.

From Juan Manuel Herrero, "Notes sobre la ideología del burgués Español del siglo xviii," *Anuario de Estudios Americanos,* IX (1952), 297–326. Used by permission of the Secretary of the editorial board, AEA.

above-mentioned classification, preroyalist or pre-Carlist. Liberal-reformists and pre-Carlists were united in opposition to the Old Regime but this opposition concealed the differences which would emerge after its overthrow.

The *Spanish Epistolario of the Eighteenth Century,* as far as it is revealed in the anthology of the Rivadeneyra collection, includes diverse and at time antagonistic ideologies, information on many subjects, and a wide range of opinion. If there is a common pattern in this intricate mosaic — one idea or sentiment that all the writers hold — it is surely love of Spain. They appealed to a love of Spain when asking for favors; they appealed to it when suggesting reforms for the common good; and they claimed it as their primary motive for engaging in intellectual and political activities. Love of Spain and preoccupation with its problems — that is the common theme. Spain was plagued with many ills, and few of them escaped the discerning eyes of these intellectuals. In general, their view of Spain was pessimistic; all about them were useless institutions, dead-letter laws, and antiquated legal processes. The libraries contained no books of recent publication, and the study of the sciences was notoriously behind the times. Agricultural production was limited and the inhabitants were in misery.

What did the intellectual do as he surveyed this discouraging scene? Did he sink into despair before the agonizing weight of these ills or did he rise to conquer them, to give new life to the country?

The intellectual of the eighteenth century was much influenced by the state of mind of this new class; he adopted the bourgeois point of view on the problems of society. "The main question," [Vicente] Rodríguez Casado wrote, "continued to be whether the new structure of society could be adapted to the Old Regime." The philosophers and jurists perceived that a new ideological cornerstone must be laid in recognition of this political fact resulting from social change. Thus what we call bour-

geois ideas were transmitted to us, not directly by the bourgeoisie, but by the intellectuals who comprehended the significance of this social change. According to bourgeois ideology, the reforms proposed by the Old Regime could only prolong the life of an outmoded political organization. What purpose could such delay serve? Some intellectuals were so pessimistic that they gave up all hope for the salvation of Spain. But these were a minority. The general tone was optimistic; there was a confidence in the future in spite of the present evils. It was difficult to be optimistic "in a nation that was so obviously decadent," but "what difficulties, what hardships, cannot be overcome by perseverance?"

The representative figure of the Old Regime was a conformist. He was profoundly pessimistic — at times so utterly pessimistic about the future of Spain that he was unwilling to see old laws amended. He was also incapable of changing his customs, which were themselves responsible for some of the ills of Spain.

Bourgeois ideology, on the other hand, was sanguine. It had faith that the nation could be revitalized by means of the new principles of reform. The bourgeoisie, fervent disciples of reform, put their trust in their own strength, in the power of their labor to subdue and transform the environment, and especially in progress and the Enlightenment — that great panacea for all ills.

The bourgeois ideology was eminently pacificist. War repelled them because it was inherently inhumane and antisocial. The bourgeoisie visualized an era of peace in which the free communication of ideas (preliberalism) and of knowledge (the Enlightenment) would permit the nation to walk boldly along the road of progress and to achieve the happiness of the greatest number of its people.

Accompanying this ideology was an admiration for foreign countries and a desire to imitate their style of civilization. Thus foreign statesmen and their methods of government were imitated; Spanish methods were held in disdain. Frederick the Great and Joseph II[3] became the models. Our system of government was ridiculed when compared with theirs. Our disorganized army, it was claimed, would have been laughed at by Frederick the Great; the empty ostentation of our court was held up in scornful contrast with that of the enlightened monarchs.

During the last years of the eighteenth century, there were intellectuals of the bourgeois ideology who eulogized the leaders of the French Revolution and the French Constituent Assembly, and praised the solutions those revolutionaries proposed for French problems, which were similar to those in Spain.

In spite of their admiration for foreign ways, the Spanish bourgeoisie of the eighteenth century did not turn their backs on Spain. They believed in the virtues of the Spanish race and held the Spanish people in great esteem. The bourgeoisie were profoundly religious and "they possessed insight and wisdom and were of all people in Europe the most capable of drafting good laws."

Deeply rooted in this ideology was the idea of affirming what was national, of showing confidence in the people and in their capacity for perfection, and of advocating the rejuvenation of our institutions by injections of the vitalizing fluid of new ideas. Their protest was against bad government and the privileged classes, who exploit the patient, uncomplaining masses. The people deserve a better life and are capable of achieving it.

The voice of these new social elements had become powerful and threatened the Old Order; and the ways of the Old Order ran in a stream bed too narrow to contain the bourgeoisie. Because these reformers regarded Spain with optimism, because they believed in her perfectibility, they were critical of her present defects and publicized reforms that were beacons lighting the path toward a better future.

Groethuysen[4] shows us the process by which the religious faith of the French bourgeoisie of the eighteenth century was either abandoned or much weakened. He says that

on the one hand, the bourgeoisie now considered that what they believed was less important, and on the other hand, they were emancipated from the ideas that dominated their thoughts and feelings because they were supported by an unquestioning faith. They now considered such an attitude unworthy of a modern bourgeoisie.

In self-conscious superiority, the bourgeoisie withdrew from the great family of the faithful. They had their own ethic. But their loss of faith was due more to convenience and to class pride than it was to conviction. Deep down, they retained a residue of faith which was displayed on certain occasions — especially in the hour of death. During most of their lifetimes, however, the easy morals of "an honest man" made them forget the obligations of a good Christian.

Thus we see the French bourgeoisie disregarding religion and even abandoning it entirely. Did the same weakening of faith occur in Spain? Was the messianic interpretation of the destiny of Spain that had been expounded in the seventeenth century to be suddenly abandoned?

The Spaniards, whether bourgeoisie or defenders of the aristocracy, who together comprised the bulwark of conservatism during the first two thirds of the century, clung to a deeply rooted faith and continued believing the supreme end of human actions to be the practice of religion and the glory of God. They put their faith into practice not only in matters directly connected with the Church but in all human activity, which should be directed toward this end. Thus, speaking of his work, Ortografía española ["Spanish Orthography"], Bordazar complained that

---

[3] Holy Roman Emperor from 1765 to 1790.

[4] Bernard Groethuysen (1880–1946), French social anthropologist.

as Pope Leo X said, an art that was invented for the glorification of God, to spread the faith, and to propagate the arts, now serves to publicize the errors of the professors of orthography.

The conservatives did not question that the clergy should preside over all manifestations of the spirit; they should direct education from earliest childhood. Conservative writers intended their books to contribute to a strengthening of the faith. Any work held in esteem contributed to the greater glory of God and to the moral perfection of society.

Piety, consequently, was what a person valued above all things. "He is very well bred," a writer said of an acquaintance, "and what is most important, he faithfully observes the sacraments."

This was an era when the Spaniard was distinguished in foreign courts by his religiosity; this demeanor also characterized the habits of the enlightened monarch, Charles III, as is evidenced by the statements of many of his contemporaries.

Morality occupied first rank as a guide to action. We find Mayans[5] crying to Heaven because "moral philosophy is the queen of the sciences, but is today excluded from the universities of Spain." In his opinion, energy had been wasted in disputes over new philosophic doctrines, energy which should have been used in the constructive labor of explaining the dogmas of Catholic moral philosophy to the students.

If this were done they would perceive the great distance that lies between virtue and vice.

The bourgeois intellectuals found it necessary to defend traditional morality from every imaginable kind of attack. Forner[6] proclaimed "that the true philosopher is concerned to show that not only in doctrine but in example vice has no place in the house of a virtuous man." This, then, is the thought and the standard of behavior of the conservative bourgeoisie. Let us see what position the liberal, reforming bourgeoisie assume toward this basic belief in the body of ideas underlying the Old Regime.

They are revealed as consistent believers. Different because of this from the contemporary French bourgeoisie, they neither knew how nor desired to abolish religion; they held it necessary that religion be a main directing force, not the main one but a very important one, in those forces guiding Spanish public life.

Their position, however, was utterly different from that of the conservative bourgeoisie. Religion interested the latter as an end and social norm; the liberal bourgeoisie were interested in religion because of its contribution to common happiness. Cabarrús, for example, spoke in laudatory terms of the priests of San Juan de Dios and the Sisters of Charity because they could care for the sick in hospitals and monasteries in a way that no one else could.

On another occasion, he recommended that religious ceremonies bless the beginning and the finishing of public works. His purpose however was purely secular — to give publicity and glory to human achievements. There can be little doubt that this was also his purpose in advising that "some monuments should be made on which the facts of this human accomplishment are inscribed."

Religion, then, became merely one element serving the common good, on the same level of importance as knowledge and philanthropy. Religion was expected to contribute to the formation of a good citizen. Moral virtues interested the liberal bourgeoisie because they support civic virtues.

Can moral virtues that rise from religious faith exist unless the nation has need of them? Or perhaps it is better to say, can religion do more than sanctify the private and public virtues of man?

[5] Gregorio Mayans y Ciscar.
[6] Juan Pablo Forner (1756–1797), Spanish satirist and scholar.

It is not true, however, that this judgment by a Spanish bourgeois implies a lack of faith. He still confessed that Providence ruled the world and believed the most perfect government must be one that most nearly governs in the image of God. If religion does not now occupy the throne as the supreme value, it is nonetheless considered one of the most important values. The liberal bourgeoisie never attacked it, and they always respected it. Even when they defended divorce as justifiable in some cases, they appealed to the authority of the Gospel.

The liberal bourgeoisie respected religious morality. They felt that such morality should be part of general law even though its maxims must be adjusted to the practical nature of the law. But they would only with great reluctance permit religious courts to enforce morality, because to do so would be to usurp the power of God. Vengeance should also be left to God.

Cabarrús clearly indicated the utilitarian character of bourgeois morality by identifying it with the outlook of the Enlightenment: "For who can doubt," he argued, "whether the closest cooperation for the common good is achieved by the pursuit of individual happiness? Who can doubt whether virtue and the enlightened love of self contribute to the same end?"

Let us note well that he is only giving definitive shape to the current idea of utilitarianism. Utilitarianism spread to the bourgeoisie of other countries; in France, for example, Groethuysen tells us that the nonbelieving bourgeoisie considered religion not only useful but necessary for the people.

This mode of thought acquired such a powerful hold on minds that the defenders of religious values had to adopt the criteria of utility in order to make their arguments convincing. Thus Padre Feijóo[7] defended virtue by showing its practical value for persons in this world. "Hypocrites will find it costs less," he said, "to practice virtue

instead of merely pretending to do so." The *Padre Maestro* appreciated the necessity of convincing a generation concerned with its material interests that the practice of virtue was the best means of advancing those interests. He was appealing to the criterion by which it measured all things.

Knowing that Feijóo argued on this basis, shall we be surprised that the bourgeoisie, the sincere, believing liberal bourgeoisie, defended religion on the altar of utilitarianism? The ship of their faith was still afloat but it had begun to leak. They were now too egotistical to strike out on a voyage with unfurled sails toward a transcendental universalist ideal; instead, they conformed to the spirit of their times by defending their faith on the grounds of its usefulness. And on the altars of utilitarianism they perhaps unconsciously sacrificed it.

This ideological position did not prevent the liberal bourgeoisie from considering themselves sincere believers and granting an important position to religion in their lives. Nor were they motivated merely by a dry utilitarianism. But they did not dare now to defend their position on other than the pragmatic principles in vogue; their reasoning was reflected in the prism of utilitarianism.

These liberal Spanish bourgeoisie who kept their faith strong, were at the same time, however, drawing ever farther from the ideology of the Old Regime. They unreservedly criticized its political organization based on the three estates.

Nor did the clergy escape their criticism. The preliberal bourgeoisie found themselves in a painful situation with respect to the clergy. Their body of ideas prompted them to attack the existing order that included this privileged social class, but because of their belief they held priests in respect.

The liberal bourgeoisie had to reconcile, if they could, their religious beliefs, which were the most vital part of their lives, with the enlightened ideas that inspired their zeal for reform. Hence the paradox in their

---

[7] Benito Jerónimo Feijóo y Montenegro (1676–1764), Spanish monk and scholar.

attitudes. On the crucial question of the position of the clergy in society, the bourgeoisie launched into diatribes against the present situation but remained respectful toward religious belief. When it came to preparing their case against the clergy, their faith did not prevent them from pointing out defects of the clergy. On the contrary, they presented a multitude of criticisms which they justified on the grounds that they were performing a positive service for the Church.

This kind of anticlericalism, based on good intentions, was not new in Spain. It could be found during the time of the Habsburgs, especially throughout the seventeenth century. Then, however, criticism of the clergy was not tinged with social protest as it was in the eighteenth century.

The critics of either century wished to protect the purity of the faith from all persons and ideas that might contaminate it; to accomplish this, they believed it necessary to correct defects in the Church wherever they might be found.

If necessary, the State should see that these defects are corrected. It should decide disputes among the clergy over chaplaincies, curacies, and property.

The State should see that priests "teach only the Gospel and what the Church orders them to teach — not what they alone think should be taught. The State should inspire these ministers of faith and morals with a holy and vigorous indignation against the many apocryphal and ridiculous religious practices that distort reason and destroy virtue. The State should see that priests endow Christianity with the sense of civilization that has made it the purest, most holy, and most useful faith for humanity.

Since the liberal bourgeoisie had a profound conviction that Christianity was the most excellent faith in the world, it is not surprising to find this conviction in their proposals for reform. They proposed that all practices manifesting an affected piety be abolished, and all aspects of religious worship be eliminated that could not be defended as manifesting a pure, evangelical spirit. It is from this point of view that they condemn certain defects in preaching that make the preacher ridiculous and ineffective, and criticize the hypocrisy in religious practices that discredits genuine piety.

The motive for their criticism of the Church was not, however, only the desire to purify the faith. Although they gave this as their reason in pointing to some defects, their motive for attacking certain others was on the grounds of usefulness to society. This was their announced motive for attacking the "false charity" that supports vagabonds and criminals.

For this same reason, they criticized what they considered the excessive number of the clergy. They were also critical for this reason of the excessive number of soldiers and public officials. But they were careful to distinguish idle, high-ranking clerics, living on stipends, from "useful and valuable workers" such as parish priests. The latter merited their respect and veneration, the former their scathing criticism as long as they were not engaged in some useful labor for society.

Guided by this same point of view, the liberal bourgeois reformers proposed that the income to the Church be redistributed, with certain parts of it going to the State. These parts included the *excusado* [a portion of the tithes], the income from Church lands and granaries, and the tax called the *Bula de Cruzada*. These proposals implied great changes in the financial system of the Church; they would result in the establishment of a fund for social aid. The reformers would also give the poor the land and other properties not needed by the Church to support its ministers. In carrying this out, however, they would see that the important purposes of the Church were respected.

In general, the bourgeois critics always showed great veneration for the Papacy even when they did not agree with papal decisions. The regular clergy, on the other hand, were the target for their shafts of anger, and clerics who taught school were especially criticized. They eulogized, however, those clerics working with the poor. They were resolutely opposed to teaching by priests because of their antiquated methods. Their attacks even reached the point of insulting those entrusted with these duties. They also scornfully criticized those persons who took minor vows so that they might pretend to be following a religious life.

They favored the parish priests, however, for the latter worked for the good of society. This usefulness won for them the esteem of the liberal bourgeoisie. The parish priests attended local meetings concerned with charity, as Cabarrús indicated:

In these meetings, a woman who has gone astray will find the road to repentance and a confidant that she can confess her sins to; these priests reconcile decorum with beneficence and moral severity with the interests of society.

To sum up, the attitude of the preliberal bourgeoisie on clerical reform was to criticize the clergy but not the Church itself. In the view of the bourgeois critics, some of the clergy were useful and respectable, others were useless and even harmful to the Church. They were dissatisfied with the present administration of ecclesiastical property.

They attacked, in short, what did not conform with their utilitarian ideas; at times, their attack was violent. But their criticism was constructive. In contrast with the French bourgeoisie who made sarcastic remarks about the least shortcomings of priests, ridiculed their lack of culture, and went to great lengths to ferret out the smallest derogatory evidence against them, the Spanish bourgeoisie wanted the priests to become enlightened so that they would form a body worthy of the influence the Church has traditionally enjoyed, and capable of acquiring even greater influence among the people.

They would then earn the respect for their personal merit that today is paid only to their position.

The clergy should not only be educated by the standards of the Enlightenment but be given authority and financial support in order to discharge their ministry in a worthy manner. This accomplished, besides their being of great usefulness to society, the Church and its ministers would merit the esteem and respect of the people.

Here, then, is the formula that reconciles the ideas of the bourgeoisie with their beliefs: reform the clergy. For what purpose? That they might serve better in the social order they themselves would help create and at the same time would be honored as individuals. This reveals the respect of the preliberal bourgeoisie for the ministers of a religion that undergirds their ideas.

We have seen the position that the bourgeoisie adopted respecting the Old Regime, their criticisms of it, and the reforms they proposed. Although these reforms were for the most part modifications of the existing order, they were in some ways the outlines for a new order that had not yet taken clear shape in their minds.

The bourgeoisie, however, had a few basic ideas which served as an understructure for their system. Convinced of the usefulness of these ideas and of their tensile strength to support an edifice of reforms, the bourgeoisie had implicit faith in their efficacy.

Among these ideas, that of the Enlightenment held a supreme position. It was a point of faith with the bourgeoisie that the Enlightenment was a panacea for all the ills of the country. The day the government became enlightened, the day it encouraged, rather than prevented, the diffusion of knowledge to all the people, on that day there would be a state of general well-being and a wave of prosperity would sweep over the nation. All citizens would feel this beneficent influence. Because of this belief, the Spanish bourgeoisie gave special attention to education and wrote long treatises on this subject. On analyzing the material found in the *Epistolario,* one finds that utilitarianism emerges clearly. That idea so suited the outlook of the bourgeoisie that it had to be included in their educational system.

The idea of utilitarianism is found in the writings of all those that refer to the Enlightenment; for example, Mayans wrote: "It seems to me that it is more important to use reason in the affairs of the world, which are so filled with the practice of sophistry, than to demonstrate great refinement of knowledge in the academic world." Cabarrús expressed this idea directly when he praised an educational system that includes only subjects useful and necessary to the State; the State, therefore, should aid those subjects that directly produce individual happiness and common prosperity.

Individual happiness and social prosperity — these are two other ideas dear to the bourgeoisie; they believed both ideas could be easily realized by an adequate education, which of itself would eliminate all obstacles. The reformers believed a complete break with the antiquated system of teaching was necessary before new pedagogical methods could be established. The universities were among the most decadent institutions. They lacked originality, produced nothing of importance, and knew nothing of true science. They would have to be replaced. "Shut them down," Cabarrús advised, "by all means shut down those universities. They are the sewers of humanity, exuding corruption and error."

Cabarrús, the avante-garde ideologist, was not the only one who took note of the sterility of pedagogy and the uselessness of its ailing organisms. Mayans, the critic, did also. More moderate in his criticism than Cabarrús, he also pointed out the defects in education and offered reforms for it.

Mayans especially wanted rational explanations to be given in teaching; he wanted problems to be explained in rational terms and demonstrations made by professors and students that were based on reason. The vapid method of offering a thesis and a counterthesis, which were usually all but unintelligible and frequently useless, should be avoided.

Cabarrús believed education should be based on the laws of nature. No blind obedience should be given, in education, to conventions of society. This would make possible the shaping of a happy individual who could pursue his self-interest except when that pursuit brought him in conflict with the interests of society as a whole. To make knowledge rational, and to diffuse it freely, were the requisites necessary to produce magic results. Cabarrús outlined the entire program when he said:

Let us purify the mind, or better, let us prevent the degradation of man's reason; let us strengthen his body; let us inspire him with love for the laws of his country, for his fellow citizens, and then let us walk forward in that light cast ahead by the combination of liberty of the press and the progress of the human spirit.

Let us analyze these postulates. A dislike of the traditional system is the first step to reach the new order. It is expressed violently in the diatribe against the universities and their methods and against the religious and their participation in education. The bourgeoisie granted that priests should be encharged with religious education, but would not tolerate them as directors of the general education of children. According to the accusation of Cabarrús, whose invective in this case is very violent, children need affection and care rather than the discipline and memory work that the priests give them.

Who are the school teachers to be? Who will direct popular education? Anyone, providing he is a "sensible, honest (that above all) humane, and patriotic man."

This patriotic idea, the main purpose of bourgeois education, went hand-in-glove with state control of education. Patriotism was included in the qualifications for teachers:

a) Must have proficiency in the rudiments of teaching: reading, writing, counting, and measuring. This is a serious obligation that society exacts from individuals; if it is not carried out, the sacred social compact is broken.

b) Must inspire the students with an affection for a "political catechism that includes learning about the society in which they live and the benefits they receive from it."

c) Must control and guide, without the use of force, the vocation of students in such way that there will be an adequate number educated in accordance with the needs of the state.

In order to achieve this end, the students were to be divided proportionately into seminaries [for student priests], schools of medicine, schools of law, etc. Special attention would be given to selecting students for professions in accordance with merit and talent. Favoritism was prohibited and consideration of the social class that the student came from was irrelevant as a basis for choice. Positions would be obtained only by passing a number of very difficult examinations; personal recommendations, which had been much relied on to the present time (as indicated in numerous letters of the *Epistolario*), would not be admitted.

General education, on the other hand, must be extended to all persons; Cabarrús proposed that agricultural schools be established as well as schools for industry and commerce. In this way the Enlightenment would reach people in the most isolated hamlets in a useful way. The result would be a visible material improvement in the country.

Cabarrús did not specify how physical education would be carried out; he gave this matter very little attention. But he mentioned diversions, advising that they were not only permissible but necessary. Instruction in games was an essential part of the educative principle.

With these elemental rules and this succint education given him, the citizen was supposed to be prepared to climb the mountain of scientific knowledge. This was to be accomplished solely by individual initiative, an effort which would be intensified by rivalry — that noble emulation which serves as a spur for the truly worthy to scale the heights to the preeminent positions in education and government.

With rivalry the stimulus to acquire an education, Cabarrús trusted in the continual advance of science to furnish its content. Nothing would be permitted to block the diffusion of knowledge. Knowledge, freely communicated, would produce ever greater progress, and with the aid of public opinion, would totally reform the new generation, which can be expected to do much good for the country.

Even in his most pessimistic moments he trusted in national education as the paramount resource.

Our people, Cabarrús believed — are not susceptible of any peaceful reform while they are ill, and since violent reform is a desperate measure, it is necessary that we direct ourselves to the new-born generation. This is the object of national education.

Because of national education, justice would temper the use of power, philanthropy would influence social relations, the sciences would progress, and a happiness, an enlightened happiness that approached Utopia, would extend its beneficent influence to all.

SUGGESTIONS FOR ADDITIONAL READING

The historiography in English for a study of Spanish America in the eighteenth century remains unsatisfactory because of its dearth and its lack of depth. There are perhaps two main reasons for this: one, that North American scholars (only a few English historians have been concerned with Latin America) have tended to concentrate on the Conquest, the Independence Period proper, and the modern revolutions; and, two, the majority of North Americans have approached Latin American history with the same assumptions and methods with which they have approached their own, being more concerned to describe and measure tangible events and processes like economic production than to deal with the ideas that have claimed the attention of Spaniards and Spanish Americans. The English-language historiography, consequently, largely concentrates upon what the civilization itself has never been predominantly concerned with. This accounts for the limited participation of North Americans in controversial historiography and suggests that North Americans and Spanish Americans have approached the latter's history from basically different philosophical positions. The North Americans have been essentially Aristotelian in the gathering of minute objective data; the Spanish Americans, on the other hand, have tended to follow the Platonic tradition in their concern with ideas and ideals. Thus, although the difference can be exaggerated, the two branches of historiography have little contact with each other and each makes a different contribution to understanding. Most of what the student reads in English is not directly relevant to the controversies discussed in this present work. It does, however, give him the facts that must be considered in judging historical interpretations and in helping him arrive at his own.

Textbooks vary greatly in treating the eighteenth century, some authors consolidating it with the colonial period as a whole in the best liberal tradition, others blending it with the Independence Period. Several recent texts, however, treat the century separately and at considerable length, two examples being Donald E. Worcester and Wendell G. Schaeffer, *The Growth and Culture of Latin America* (New York, 1956), and John Edwin Fagg, *Latin America, A General History* (New York, 1963). Briefer interpretive treatments can be found in the introduction to R. A. Humphreys and John Lynch, eds., *The Origins of the Latin American Revolutions, 1808–1826* (New York, 1965), and in an earlier article by Humphreys, "The Fall of the Spanish American Empire," *History*, XXXVII, New Series (February-October, 1952), 213–227. An older but still valuable interpretation for its suggestiveness of historical continuity is an article by Victor A. Belaunde, "Factors of the Colonial Period in South America Working toward a New Regime," *Hispanic American Historical Review (HAHR)* IX, No. 2 (May, 1929), 144–153. Although there is no general work that unites Spanish reform programs with their implementation in America, the student can learn much by analogy from Richard Herr's *The Eighteenth-Century Revolution in Spain* (Princeton, 1958). The older works by Bernard Moses, *South America on the Eve of Independence* (New York, 1908), and *Spain's Declining Power in South America, 1730–1806* (Berkeley, 1919), suffer from a superficial liberalist interpretation; a later general work by a provocative Spanish liberal, Salvador de Madariaga, *The Fall of the Spanish American Empire* (New York, 1947) is likely to seem too discursive until much detail has been assimilated from other works.

Aside from these general works, the student is obliged to turn to monographs limited by region, subject matter, and time for an appreciation of political reforms. An excellent recent work by John Lynch, *Spanish Colonial Administration, 1782–1810; The Intendant System in the Viceroyalty of the Río de la Plata* (London, 1958) reveals not only the practice as opposed to theory of the intendancy system but revises the traditional concept of the politically stagnant *cabildos*. Another intensively researched study of Bourbon government in practice is *The Viceregency of Antonio María Bucareli in New Spain* (Austin, 1962) by Bernard E. Bobb. Herbert I. Priestley covers in great detail the general reforms in New Spain in *José de Gálvez, Visitor-General of New Spain (1765–1771)* (Berkeley, 1916); similar reforms in Peru have received only brief treatment by Eunice Joiner Gates, "Don José Antonio de Areche: His Own Defense," *HAHR*, VIII, No. 1 (February, 1928), 14–42, and Lillian Estelle Fisher, "Teodoro de Croix," *HAHR*, IX, No. 4 (November, 1929), 488–504. Miss Fisher has also presented a somewhat theoretical treatment of the intendancy system in *The Intendant System in Spanish America* (Berkeley, 1929). Spanish plans for reorganizing the Spanish American Empire have been reviewed by A. S. Aiton, "Spanish Colonial Reorganization under the Family Compact," *HAHR*, XII, No. 3 (August, 1932), 269–280. Descriptions of international rivalry involving and testing the state of Bourbon preparedness can be gleaned from Richard Pares, *War and Trade in the West Indies, 1739–1763* (New York, 1936); Dauril Alden, "The Undeclared War of 1773–1777: Climax of Luso-Spanish Platine Rivalry," *HAHR*, XLI, No. 1 (February, 1960), 55–74; and Charles E. Nowell, "The Defense of Cartagena," *HAHR*, XLII, No. 4 (November, 1962), 477–501.

Bourbon economic reforms have been typically approached by describing British and later United States commercial penetration of Spanish America. The following articles are representative: Vera Lee Brown's "The South Sea Company and Contraband Trade," *American Historical Review*, XXXI (1926), 662–678, and "Contraband Trade: A Factor in the Decline of Spain's Empire in America," *HAHR*, VIII, No. 2 (May, 1928), 178–189. And, in the same vein, Roy F. Nichols, "Trade Relations and the Establishment of the United States Consulates in Spanish America, 1779–1809," *HAHR*, XIII, No. 3 (August, 1933), 289–313; Allan Christelow, "Contraband Trade Between Jamaica and the Spanish Main, and the Free Port Act of 1766," *HAHR*, XXII, No. 2 (May, 1942), 309–343, and "Great Britain and the Trades from Cádiz and Lisbon to Spanish America and Brazil, 1759–1783," *HAHR*, XXVII, No. 1 (February, 1947), 2–29. Studies of the Spanish American economy itself in relation to Bourbon reforms include: Roland D. Hussey, *The Caracas Company, 1728–1784* (Cambridge, 1934), and two articles by Troy S. Floyd, "The Guatemalan Merchants, the Government, and the Provincianos, 1750–1800," *HAHR*, XLI, No. 1 (February, 1961), 90–110, and "Bourbon Palliatives and the Central American Mining Industry," *The Americas*, XVIII, No. 2 (October, 1961), 103–125.

The intellectual awakening of the creoles during the eighteenth century has received only limited attention from North Americans, most of whom assumed that the first task was to refute the Black Legend by demonstrating that Spanish Americans had the capacity and the opportunity for Enlightenment. Such a view limits the value of *Latin America and the Enlightenment* (New York, 1942, 1961), edited by Arthur P. Whitaker; nonetheless it is a useful introduction to the subject. John Tate Lanning's *The Eighteenth-Century Enlightenment in the University of San Carlos de Guatemala* (Ithaca, 1956) removed the last doubt that creoles were "abreast of the current ideas," as did Robert J. Shafer's *The Economic Societies in the Spanish World (1763–1821)* (Syracuse, 1958). In the assessment of more specific influences, J. R.

Spell treats the impact on Spanish Americans of a notable Frenchman in *Rousseau in the Spanish World before 1833* (Austin, 1938). Few Spanish American intellectuals have received more than exploratory treatment in a few articles. Lillian Estelle Fisher has studied the Spanish priest and reformer in Mexico in a work entitled *Champion of Reform, Manuel Abad y Queipo* (New York, 1955). A specialized but valuable treatment of the application of useful knowledge by creoles is that by Clement G. Motten, *Mexican Silver and the Enlightenment* (Philadelphia, 1950).

The effects of the military reforms in New Spain can be appreciated from Lyle N. McAlister's *The "Fuero Militar" in New Spain, 1764–1800* (Gainesville, 1957). The conflicting interpretations of the expulsion of the Jesuits, together with wider assessments of the Jesuits' impact on Spanish American civilization, can be obtained from *The Expulsion of the Jesuits from Latin America* (New York, 1965), edited by Magnus Mörner.

2 3 4 5 6 7 8

PROBLEMS
IN LATIN AMERICAN
CIVILIZATION

Heath